■SCHOLASTIC

Guided Reading in Grades 3–6

Everything You Need to Make Small-Group Reading Instruction Work in Your Classroom

---✴---

Mary Browning Schulman

New York • Toronto • London • Auckland • Sydney
Mexico City • New Delhi • Hong Kong • Buenos Aires   **Teaching** *Resources*

KH

Dedication

To Charlie, my brother and friend

Acknowledgments

Some of the best things in this book, and the book itself, couldn't have been done without the help and contribution of many. I have been deeply influenced by the children, teachers, and administrators I work with in my district in Fairfax County, Virginia. I would like to thank the many teachers at Annandale Terrace, McNair Elementary, and Woodley Hills for so graciously opening their classroom doors to share their time, students, ideas, and materials. In particular, I am grateful to Liz Cummings, Amy Dywer, Amy Green, Maddie Leon, Jennifer Orr, Jill Silton, Dak Smith, Lisa Stern, Jamie Stafford, and Michelle Zimmerman.

I'd also like to acknowledge the Title I office staff in Fairfax County, who provided ongoing moral support during the writing of this book. I am especially grateful to Barbara Blevins, literacy collaborative trainer, and Noël Naylor, Reading Recovery teacher leader, for many stimulating conversations about teaching and children's learning about reading as well as for reading portions of the manuscript and providing valuable feedback. Thanks also go to Dianne Napolitano, Reading Recovery teacher leader, who passed on numerous timely and helpful articles.

I am fortunate to once again live and work in a school environment on a daily basis. London Towne Elementary is a school that hums with collegial and collaborative energy, which truly enriches and elevates the workplace and the teaching and learning that happens there with all students. A special thanks to principal Andrew Camarda and assistant principal Sigrid Ryberg, who invited me to work with teachers and students at London Towne even before I joined the staff. I am also grateful to Sigrid for reading an early draft of the manuscript and making suggestions on how to make it better. In particular, I would like to thank the following London Towne friends and colleagues: Shele Banford, E.J. Green, Jason Hardy, Rachel King, Ray Lonnett, Keith Matias, Dana Moury, Jason Pannutti, and Lisa Washington for sharing their classroom stories so I could capture in this book some of the teaching and learning that happens with their students. A special thanks to Shannon Lewis for all the fine recommendations of books for children. I'd also like to thank reading resource teachers Tania Dedham and Jessica Howell for demonstrating their own teaching and for the many good "teaching conversations"—I walked away each time richer from them.

My heartfelt thanks go to my dear friends and colleagues Carleen Payne and Pat Johnson for reading and rereading the manuscript along its long road to the end—even in the midst of working on their own manuscripts. I so appreciate your time and insightful questions, ideas, suggestions, and nudges along the way. You both never fail to inspire my thinking.

I thank my publisher, Scholastic, which has supported my efforts along the way. I especially thank editor Joanna Davis-Swing for her guidance, patience, and help throughout the writing of this book. Thanks to Sarah Morrow for her wonderful graphic design work. I'd also like to thank Terry Cooper, vice president/editor-in-chief, Scholastic Teaching Resources.

I am especially grateful to my family and their ongoing love, belief, and support. You make coming home for visits the best of times. A special thanks to Charles Browning, my brother and family wordsmith, who by the reading and rereading of many drafts helped bring greater clarity and understanding to the pages. To Lucille Schulman, who has a strength of will I admire, thank you for the times you cheered me on. And to Jay, the guy who makes living life the best of times, my deepest thanks for taking the photographs for the book, your unconditional support, encouragement, and love. You truly changed my life the moment you entered it.

✳

Cover design by Adana Jiminez
Interior design by Sarah Morrow

Copyright © 2006 by Mary Browning Schulman
All rights reserved. Published by Scholastic Inc.
Printed in the U.S.A.
ISBN-13 978-0-439-44397-5
ISBN-10 0-439-44397-0

9/19/06

1 2 3 4 5 6 7 8 9 10   40   12 11 10 09 08 07 06

Contents

Introduction

If we want our intermediate students to be readers, it makes sense that a large portion of their time should be spent doing just that—reading. Most likely, many of our intermediate students can already read. Still, we cannot assume students come to us fully equipped with the strategies and skills they need to read the more challenging texts they are now encountering.

Guided reading is one instructional technique you can use to help your students develop independent reading strategies so they can process and understand a variety of more demanding texts. In guided reading, four to six students actively read and problem-solve their way through a text selected by the teacher. Guided reading brings about real opportunities for constructing meaning, reflection, and insights as the teacher and a small group of students talk, read, and think their way purposefully through a new text. As Margaret Mooney writes in *Reading To, With, and By Children* (1990), in guided reading "the teacher uses questions and comments to help children become aware of resources within themselves and in the text which will enable them to overcome difficulties" in reading. Guided reading is an approach that is appropriate at all levels—from emergent readers to the most capable upper-grade students. This book focuses on the use of guided reading with students in grades 3–6.

Over the years teachers I've worked with have asked me where they could find short guided reading text selections for use with older readers. "I don't have time to search out pieces for my students to read," they would say. I write this book for those teachers and all others who may be in search of short guided reading texts that can be easily reproduced for students. Most of the text selections included in this book can be read with students in one or two guided reading sessions.

The reproducible texts offered in this book range from easier to harder-to-read texts so you can identify those that are best suited for your instructional purposes and your students' range of reading abilities. The text selections include fiction, folktales, and content-related topic pieces. The content-related texts link to real-world experiences and elicit a wide range of interests, responses, and opinions. A variety of text structures and features in the selections also offer students repeated occasions to learn how different texts work and are organized, and give rise to discussions of how the structures and features assist readers as they navigate the passage.

You may want to consider enlarging a text selection on an overhead transparency to model fluent reading and strategy use specific to the learning needs of a group of students (Holdaway, 1984; Parkes, 2000; Brown, 2004; Payne, 2005).

Here's What You'll Find in This Book

In Chapter 1, I explain what guided reading is and why we use it in the intermediate grades to support the teaching of reading. Chapter 2 focuses on assessment. The assessment information collected and analyzed enables you to do a better job of grouping, planning, and teaching what students need to learn next.

In Chapter 3, I share a lesson design and framework for planning and teaching guided reading lessons. In Chapter 4, I explain how readers actively use a system of comprehension strategies to understand the texts they are reading. Chapter 5 presents ways of laying the groundwork for creating a reading workshop. And in Chapter 6, I step into intermediate classrooms to take a look at examples of actual guided reading lessons with older readers.

The goal of guided reading is to help students become stronger, more independent, confident, competent, and discriminating readers who actively think while they read and can discuss new texts critically. This book will offer you some practical and useful ideas to help implement guided reading with your intermediate students. I invite you now to have a closer look at the teaching of reading—guided reading in particular.

Chapter 1

Mary meets with a group of third-grade students to read and learn more about nonfiction text features during guided reading.

Guided Reading: What It Is and How It Fits Into a Comprehensive Literacy Framework

Guided reading is an enabling and empowering approach where the focus is on the child as the long-term learner being shown how and why and which strategies to select and employ to ensure that meaning is gained and maintained during the reading and beyond.

—Margaret Mooney, *Reading To, With, and By Children*

Guided reading is an instructional approach that gives you an opportunity to tailor direct instruction to students' specific reading needs and to help deepen their understanding and processing of a wide variety of texts. It is an approach that is appropriate for all levels of readers—from the primary-level reader to the most capable intermediate reader. During guided reading the teacher *guides* and *supports* students, usually in a small-group setting, as "they talk, read, and think their way purposely through" a text (New Zealand Ministry of Education, 1997, page 80) selected by the teacher. The selected text provides just enough challenge to slightly stretch students as they practice using their reading strategies and problem-solving skills with guidance from the teacher.

Guided reading is the perfect opportunity for you to help students practice the reading strategies and skills you have demonstrated and explained during read-alouds and shared reading experiences. Let's take a look at a guided reading lesson in a third-grade classroom to see the rich teaching and learning that can occur during a well-planned session.

A Guided Reading Lesson in Action

It's mid-morning. I'm gathered around a table with a group of four third-grade students ready to begin a guided reading lesson during reading workshop. I've selected a nonfiction book titled *Deserts*. The students and I have been learning about the desert in our science study, and because this is a current topic of study, I know students will be able to bring background knowledge to the reading. In addition, during read-alouds and shared reading we've been talking about how authors use nonfiction text features such as a table of contents, headings, and photographs with captions to organize a text for the reader, and *Deserts* contains all of these. From the assessment information I gathered on these struggling readers, I know that this particular book will permit them to read for meaning, draw on the skills they already control, and actively use their current processing strategies. The text presents only a few challenges so they will not need to spend large amounts of time trying to figure out words and/or their meaning.

The book uses a question-and-answer structure. Knowing the text structure will help students anticipate what's to come and support them as they make meaning while reading.

Before Reading: Tune In to the Text

Before reading is the time to motivate and prepare the students for reading. My purpose for reading in today's lesson is twofold. First, I plan to guide and support the students as they read and use the nonfiction features in the text to understand how the book is organized. And second, I will help the students determine what information is new and what information they already know as they read the text. I've given each student a copy of the book and we engage in the following discussion before reading.

Supporting All Students

It's important for all students to have opportunities to meet with you to refine and extend their reading comprehension strategies and skills. Struggling readers and English language learners (ELLs) need more guidance and more supported instruction than other students. Consider meeting with them in guided reading groups and/or individual reading conferences almost every day. Students who are reading at grade level will not need to meet in guided reading groups every day unless the focus of instruction for a particular small group requires meeting on a more consistent basis for a short time. Higher-achieving students may meet with you only for a quick checkup because they can do more on their own.

Mrs. S.: Readers, I have a new nonfiction book for you to read. The title is *Deserts* and it's by Margie Burton, Cathy French, and Tammy Jones. Take a look at the cover and title and think about what we've been learning about deserts in science. (*I pause briefly for the students to read the title and look at the photo on the front cover.*) In today's lesson, we're going to look at how authors organize nonfiction books to help the reader. Then, since we've been talking about deserts and desert life in science, we're going to read to find out if we can learn any new information about deserts. Take a minute or so to preview your book to see how the authors organized it. As you look, ask yourself: How did the authors organize the book to make it easier for us to read the information about deserts? (*I point to this question, which I've written ahead of time on the whiteboard. Students open their books and begin to preview on their own. I observe, making notes about how and where students look while previewing the book.*)

What did you notice about the way the book is organized for the reader?

Cameron: It has a table of contents at the beginning so you know what they're going to tell you about the desert—all the different things or topics.

Jonah: They're all questions. And they put the pages where you go to find the answers. I looked at the questions in the table of contents. Like here it says, "Do animals live in the desert?" (*He points to the table of contents.*) Then I went to page 10 and saw that it talked about the animals that live in the desert.

The selected text allows students to use their background knowledge to access information and offers appropriate conceptual and reading challenges. My introduction

- *introduces title, genre, and author.*
- *gives students a purpose for today's reading.*
- *gives students the responsibility to preview how the authors organized the text by skimming and scanning on their own.*

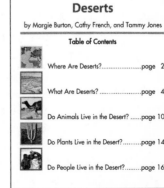

Deserts

by Margie Burton, Cathy French, and Tammy Jones

Table of Contents

Where Are Deserts?......................page 2

What Are Deserts? ....page 4

Do Animals Live in the Desert? ......page 10

Do Plants Live in the Desert?..........page 14

Do People Live in the Desert?.........page 16

During this time, I

- *record student observations.*
- *explore students' understanding of nonfiction features in text.*

Mrs. S.: So both of you checked the beginning of the book for a table of contents. Cameron, you mentioned the table of contents helps the reader know what important information related to the big topic of deserts will be in the book. Let's check that out. Turn to the table of contents and read that page. If you already read it when you previewed the book, read through it quickly again. (*Students turn to the table of contents and read silently.*)

So, from the table of contents, do we have a good idea which topics will be in the book?

Cameron: Yes, it'll tell us where the deserts are and what they are.

Kim: And if plants, animals, and people live there.

Mrs. S.: So now we have a good idea which specific topics we'll read about in the book. Jonah, you noticed that the authors used questions. Then you looked to see if they would answer them, and you found out they did. Readers, do you see how the authors used questions throughout the table of contents? Let's find the question Jonah mentioned—Do animals live in the desert? (*I give students a moment to skim the table of contents again.*) And as Jonah said, the place where the authors answer that question starts on page 10. Kim mentioned plants and people. Find the questions the authors ask about both of those topics and the pages where we'll read about them. (*Students find the questions and the pages.*) Okay, on our chart titled "Important Nonfiction Text Features," I'll write "table of contents," "topics with page numbers," and "question-and-answer format." (*I begin a list of nonfiction features that signal importance to the reader.*) What else did you notice during your previewing of the book?

Tia: There are maps and photographs of real animals and places.

Mrs. S.: Let's add both of those ideas to our list. But first, Tia, did you notice anything under the photographs to help the reader? (*Tia looks in the book to check.*)

Tia: Yes, there are words under it that tell about the picture. I forget what they're called, but they're blue.

Cameron: I think they're called captions.

Mrs. S.: Say more about captions.

Cameron: Captions tell you important information about the picture.

Mrs. S.: Yes. (*I pause, waiting for Cameron to say more.*)

Cameron: The author puts them in a nonfiction book so you can learn more about what it is you're reading about . . . if you look at the picture and read the caption.

Mrs. S.: That's right. A group of words that is under, beside, or above a picture is called a caption. Just as Cameron said, the caption tells you important information about the picture. It gives you more information than the picture by itself. Turn to page 15 and read the caption at the bottom. (*Students read the caption silently. Some pause at the word* baobab *in the caption.*) Did you figure out the word that tells what kind of tree it is?

Jonah: I think it's *ba . . . o . . . bab*—a baobab tree.

Here I

- *help students construct an understanding of features in nonfiction.*
- *ask students to reread to confirm.*
- *give responsibility to students to search for specific topics.*

Now, I

- *confirm question-answer text structure.*
- *draw attention and elaborate on the question-answer text structure in the table of contents.*
- *prompt students to use the table of contents to locate information.*

At this point I begin generating a list of nonfiction text features with students to reinforce their understanding of how nonfiction conventions help the reader sift essential information from less important information.

Mrs. S.: That's right. It helps to look at the parts of longer words. Jonah figured out it has three parts—*ba . . . o . . . bab*. And then he put it together by looking at the whole word. Did anyone else do that? (*Two other students respond yes.*) Let's say that word together. (*Students say word.*) In your reading you may come to other longer words where you will need to look at the parts to figure them out. We'll talk about those words after you read. So, what do we know about the baobab tree from the caption?

Tia: It has really deep roots so it can find water.

Mrs. S.: Yes, that's one thing we know about this tall tree that lives in the desert. And notice how the words in the caption under the photo of the baobab tree are in blue so they stand out. They're saying, "Read this. This information is important!" That's exactly what you thought, Tia, isn't it? (*I add "maps," "photographs," "captions," and "color print" to the list.*)

   Anything else we should add to the chart?

Kim: There are headings on some of the pages.

Mrs. S.: Say more about what you noticed about those headings, Kim.

Kim: Well, the headings are questions and the letters are bigger and blacker.

Mrs. S.: Kim is on page 14. Let's all turn to that page. See how she noticed the heading at the top? And how it's written as a question—just like in the table of contents? That tells you what this part will be about. Notice how the letters are bigger and darker. We call the dark letters "boldface" print. Why did the authors use larger letters and boldface print in the headings?

Kim: I think so it'd stand out for the reader.

Mrs. S.: Exactly. The way they wrote it says, "Look here, this is important. Pay attention because this part is going to tell you if plants live in the desert." See how much we learn as readers just by noticing the way the authors organized the book and used special features to signal important parts? Remember, readers, we need to pay attention to these things before we read and while we're reading. (*I add "headings" and "boldface print" to the chart.*)

   Now that you've looked at how the book is organized, I want you to think about what you already know about deserts. Think about all our discussions during science and what you've learned. Turn and talk to your elbow partner for a minute or so about what you know about deserts. (*I give students about 60–75 seconds to turn and talk. I jot down ideas I hear the partners discuss. Then I ask each student to relate something their partner told them about deserts.*)

   All right, as you read this book on your own, I want you to think about what you already know about deserts—what you just told your partner or

Notice how I

- *bring out important vocabulary.*
- *draw attention to how breaking a word into parts can help students read it.*
- *remind students to look at the parts of a longer word to solve it while reading.*
- *probe for information accessed from caption.*
- *draw attention to a text feature—font—and its effect—to signal important information.*
- *reinforce understanding of heading, boldface print, and font size.*

At this point in the lesson, I

- *show what a reader might be thinking when noticing headings in text.*
- *provide opportunities for students to refine their understandings of how nonfiction features and text structure help the reader as they're reading to determine what's important.*
- *encourage students to use their background knowledge to anticipate the information they will find and share with a partner.*
- *support students' learning through social interaction and dialogue with one another.*

what you heard when we shared. I also want you to pay attention to when you learn something new about deserts in your reading. If you read something new, I want you to flag it with a sticky-note. So, in your head while you're reading you might be saying, "Yes, I know that. Oh, and I know that about deserts." But then you'll be reading along and you'll say, "Oh, that's new information. I didn't know that about deserts." That's when you'll flag the book with a sticky-note. Notice which nonfiction text features help you as you read, too. (*I give each student a sticky-note precut into five strips that they can tear off to flag new information.*)

Readers, when you're finished reading, we'll talk about what you read, what you already knew, and where you noticed that you learned something new about deserts. If you finish early, go back and reread the passages you flagged with sticky-notes, so you'll be ready to talk about them. Okay, turn to page 2 and begin reading silently on your own.

Students and I generated a list of the nonfiction text features. We referred to the list both before and after reading other nonfiction texts during the next few guided reading lessons. We added to the chart any new nonfiction text features students encountered in the texts they read. I placed a tally mark next to the text features students found in each of the subsequent nonfiction texts. Then we used the chart to compare and contrast one nonfiction text with another and discussed which text features were most often used by authors to support readers navigating nonfiction texts.

Important nonfiction text
features in the book *Deserts*

- title
- table of contents
- topics with page numbers
- question-and-answer format
- maps
- photographs with captions
- color print
- headings
- boldface print
- larger print or font

During Reading: Read the Text

Students remain at the table to read the book on their own silently. While they read, I confer briefly with two students individually. When I touch a student's shoulder, it's a signal to begin to softly read aloud. I take notes on what the students are doing as they process the text. I record reading behaviors exhibited when they encounter difficulty, strategies they use as they read, and whether the reading is phrased and fluent. At times I may help an individual reader solve a difficult word or briefly discuss the text. In this particular lesson, I often exchanged quick comments about a part where the student flagged something newly learned.

After Reading: Return to the Focus and Dig Deeper to Extend Thinking About the Text

Next, students share the places in the book where they flagged new learning. Most students have identified three or four places. The students take turns directing others to places in the book they've flagged. They notice some of the information

"Turn and Talk"
Conversation Technique

Developing relationships and partnerships among students is important in the classroom. Providing opportunities for students to stop, turn toward a partner knee-to-knee, and take turns talking not only helps develop those relationships but it also gives them a chance to learn from one another. The "turn and talk" technique can be used at many points during whole-group and small-group instruction. It works well during read-alouds and during shared, guided, and independent reading when you want students to respond to a text they've heard or read or to a common experience.

To introduce the technique, model it with a student. Then allow students to practice the turn and talk structure with a partner. Make sure students understand their shifting role as both listener and speaker. You may find it helpful to signal the beginning and end of turn and talk in a predictable way with a shaker, chimes, bells, or a clapper.

When students are talking, circulate among the partners to listen briefly to the conversations. If you notice partners having difficulty getting started, you may restate the focus to jump-start the conversation. It's okay to honor tentative responses. Often students who are shy or are second-language learners need support in getting conversations started. You may wish to pair students who speak the same first language so that the stronger of the two can help facilitate the talk through their native language.

As you listen in, you can take anecdotal notes and use that information to decide who might share when the group comes together again. It's not necessary for all students to share with the class; select a few representative partners. You may ask students to share what they said or what their partner told them. Make it a positive experience and allow partners to help each other. The turn and talk technique permits students to process what they hear, read, or experience; share their thinking; and learn from one another in a nonthreatening, supportive context.

they flagged is new to all of them. As they share this new information, many of the students discuss what they already knew and how what they've learned fits into their current understandings. I quickly write the items they've identified as "new learning" on a piece of chart paper so everyone can see the different ideas. Kim is particularly surprised by what she read in one of the captions about the nighttime temperature in some deserts dropping below freezing, and realizes she has to adjust her thinking based on new information she's read. She says, "I used to think deserts were always hot. Then I read here that's not always true. Now I have to change what I think about deserts. I learned some deserts, like the Gobi Desert, can get really cold at night."

Mary listens to one student read a small portion of the text in the guided reading lesson during reading. She jots down anecdotal notes of what she observes.

Cameron talks about learning the name of a new animal, the *addax*, that lives in the desert. He mentions how he had to slow down to figure the word out and solved it by breaking it into parts. Another unexpected fact students come across in their reading is that people live in the desert. Their conversation leads to a series of wonderings about how people survive in the desert. Some of their questions are: How do people get out of the heat? What kinds of homes do they have? How do they get their food? How do they keep from getting sunburned? Students decide they want to find out more about people who make their home in the desert. We make plans to look for books in the school library and search the Internet.

As we end the guided reading lesson, I remind students that whenever they're reading nonfiction, it's important to preview the text to see how the author organized it and to look for any special features that signal something important to the reader. I also remind students to think about what they already know before reading and during reading, and to pay special attention when they learn something new.

Summary of the Guided Reading Lesson

For this guided reading lesson I selected a text that would permit students to use their background knowledge to access information throughout their first reading. It offered a manageable number of conceptual and reading challenges for this group of struggling readers. I introduced the text, involving the students in a discussion about nonfiction text features, and had them engage in collaborative partner talk to activate background knowledge. All students assumed the reader's role by reading the text individually. The group discussed the new information they learned.

> Nonfiction is one of the most accessible genres for reluctant and less experienced readers because the features scaffold the reader's understanding.
>
> —Stephanie Harvey and Ann Goudvis, *Strategies That Work*

The introduction took about six minutes. Students read the 16-page book and flagged new learning in about seven minutes. The discussion following the reading took about another eight minutes. So, in about 21 minutes, students learned some basic tenets about how authors use nonfiction conventions to organize information in a text to assist readers. For example, students learned about

- reading the table of contents to determine specific topics in the book.

- noticing text formats like question-and-answer.

- reading captions with photographs.

- noticing boldface headings and other typographical effects that signal importance.

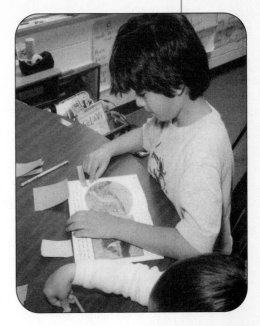

Students practiced and applied what they'd learned as they each read the whole text. They discussed their new understandings and became interested in further investigation and reading about the topic. The next guided reading text for the students in this group will be another one that interests and motivates them and supports further reading development and an understanding of nonfiction features.

Students flag places in the text that show new learning. Students share what they learned in the after-reading discussion.

Why and How Do We Use Guided Reading in the Intermediate Grades?

To address the "why" part of this question, it may help to think of reading as a continuum. As readers travel along the reading continuum throughout their elementary school life, they encounter new and increasingly challenging texts. Most primary students acquire the basics about reading and the processing of text. As students move into the intermediate grades, they continue to need support in reading. They need to learn how to process increasingly complex demands of text—especially when faced with texts that introduce new concepts, content-specific vocabulary, or complex language structures. Guided reading provides the following:

- an approach that you can use to support and to meet the needs of intermediate students as they progress and encounter increasingly challenging texts

- an opportunity for you to introduce students to texts that are accessible and comprehensible, and that offer occasions to extend their reading ability and learn

- a powerful way to reinforce and to explicitly teach as necessary multiple reading strategies and skills that you ultimately want students to use on their own during independent reading

The goal of guided reading, then, is to help students, wherever they happen to be on the reading continuum, become better, more independent readers so they can successfully construct meaning as they read new texts and discuss them critically afterward.

Most intermediate students who have moved beyond the early, "learning to read" stage are developing competence and experience as readers of increasingly demanding texts. Therefore, the "how" of guided reading instruction in the intermediate grades necessarily differs to some degree from instruction in the primary grades. In a class of 25 students, there may be four or five guided reading groups. You may want to meet with two of them for 15–25 minutes each during an hour-long workshop period while the other students in the class read independently. On some days, you may choose to hold individual reading conferences instead of guided reading groups. It's important to remain flexible and think about which teaching approach—small-group guided reading or individual reading conferences—will most benefit your students in their reading instruction. To read more about scheduling reading workshop time to include both guided reading and individual reading conferences, see Chapter 5.

The decisions you make with regard to small-group instruction—the number of groups, type of groups, size of the groups, number of days, and what to teach—will always depend on the needs of your students. In the intermediate grades, when you consider grouping students for guided reading, think beyond grouping solely by ability. You may wish to form and re-form guided reading groups based on any of the following criteria:

- **Ability**—Groups are formed according to similar reading ability. Books are matched to the readers' instructional level; texts provide sufficient supports and manageable challenges for students to read successfully, and to move forward.

- **Specific need/focused task**—Groups are formed according to similar needs. Explicit instruction is given to help readers learn what they need to know next in order to move forward, such as how to select appropriate books, read punctuation, preview a book, and so on.

- **Reading strategies**—Groups are formed to explore reading strategies— the "in the head" processes that readers use to build meaning and understanding when reading, such as monitoring, self-correcting, visualizing, and so on. (For more on reading strategies, see Chapter 4.)

- **Interest**—Groups are formed according to similar interests. Focus may include topic, genre, series, or authors readers care about and want to pursue further—such as sharks, mystery, Roald Dahl, and so on. (For more on determining students' reading interests, see Reading Log, pages 37–38)

When forming and re-forming groups, think about which students have common needs, skills, or interests, and would benefit from similar instruction. Meeting with small groups of four to six students is time efficient and an effective way to teach. Groups will change from time to time as students develop and as their interests shift. Thus, the membership of the guided reading groups needs to remain flexible. (To read more about how one teacher makes decisions about grouping students in his classroom, see pages 44–47.)

A Comprehensive Literacy Framework Supports Student Learning

Guided reading is a powerful approach that teachers can use to develop literacy learning and to deepen students' understanding of a wide range of texts; keep in mind, however, that guided reading is only one component of a comprehensive literacy framework. As you will see in later chapters, guided reading is not introduced until the other parts of the framework are in place. However, guided reading does not replace other parts of the reading framework. To meet the diverse needs of your students, you will necessarily use a variety of approaches in your teaching of reading all year long. Read-alouds, shared reading, literature study groups, and partner and independent reading, used in conjunction with guided reading, are all a part of the reading instructional program in intermediate classrooms.

Literacy opportunities in intermediate classrooms include reading to, with, and by students and writing to, with, and by students (Mooney, 1990). These opportunities offer a range of support from the teacher: those in which learners receive a high degree of support through modeling and other assistance, including read-alouds, modeled writing, and shared reading and writing; those in which students receive a lower degree of support, including guided and independent reading and writing.

All of the approaches in a comprehensive literacy framework are equally important; that doesn't mean, however, that the time you spend on each of the approaches will be equal. The time you commit to the approaches will vary depending on the understanding, experiences, attitudes, and expectations your students bring to their reading. For example, at the beginning of the school year, you will give the bulk of your reading workshop time to read-alouds, shared reading, and independent reading. Once you assess students to determine their interests, abilities, and experiences, you can group students according to similar needs and thus dedicate much of your reading workshop to guided reading. For more on assessment see Chapter 2.

> *W*hen we teachers understand the learning model, we begin to make different decisions. We recognize teaching as 'a powerful, invitational relationship that pulls the learner in.' . . .we think about teaching in terms of our students' needs and interests.
>
> —Regie Routman, *Reading Essentials*

In the charts on pages 18–21, I've highlighted the various reading components of a comprehensive literacy framework that supports students' literacy learning in reading. (Note that although comprehensive literacy instruction encompasses both reading and writing, throughout this book I will be talking only about reading instruction. For a graphic overview of how these reading components fit within a complete and comprehensive reading/writing literacy framework, see inside back cover.

The Reading Components of a

HIGH TEACHER SUPPORT

Reading To

Literacy opportunities in E.J. Green's fifth-grade classroom include reading to, with, and by students. E.J. decides which learning approach in the comprehensive literacy framework will best deliver the focus of instruction in reading. Here are the reading components he uses to support literacy learning in reading.

When introducing or highlighting a strategy for the first time, E.J. demonstrates for his fifth-grade students how a reader uses the strategy. Here he shows how a reader makes inferences during a read-aloud of a picture book.

Reading With

E.J. often plans and selects texts for guided reading that will echo and support the focus of instruction in previous read-alouds and shared reading lessons. Students read and discuss inferences after reading a content-related text in this guided reading lesson.

Once students gain some understanding of the strategy, E.J. assists his fifth-grade students as they try it out. Here he supports students as they make inferences during the shared reading of a lifted text.

Read-alouds and **shared reading** experiences provide students with frequent models and demonstrations of the strategies and skills readers and writers use. Both help students construct meaning and develop comprehension with a more expert reader, the teacher. Read-alouds and shared reading experiences present students with important opportunities to both observe and question the teacher about being a reader. In addition, they are chances for the teacher to show her thinking and understanding through the use of think-alouds. During read-alouds and shared reading students depend on the teacher to model, explain, show them how to "do" the reading work, and provide support as they participate on a limited basis.

In **guided reading**, we hand over to students more of the responsibility for reading and constructing meaning of texts. Students individually and often silently read texts selected by the teacher. As they read, we expect them to practice what they've learned about being a strategic reader of texts. We teach as necessary, facilitate discussion, clarify, and support students while they apply what they've learned as readers. By bringing what we've demonstrated during read-alouds and/or shared reading to guided reading, we better focus and connect our instruction so that students are able to reinforce their learning in a variety of ways.

Comprehensive Literacy Framework

Reading With

E.J. meets with members of a literature study group while they discuss the book they are reading.

Literature study group members select a shared book to read. The group meets once to a few times each week to discuss the agreed-upon assigned reading of the text. Students are expected to come to the study session prepared for an in-depth conversation about the reading. At times, study group members may write about an event or issue, which becomes the catalyst for conversation. The teacher is often a part of the study group; however, as students become more familiar with its structure, they may facilitate the group at times.

Two fifth-grade students partner-read a book of poetry to practice phrasing and fluency before spending time reading independently.

During **partner reading**, students come together to read and talk in ways that support their understanding of a common text. Additionally, partner reading time can be used to support fluency, decoding, and comprehension, and to build reading stamina.

Reading By

Students spend 35–45 minutes each day reading a self-selected "just right" text or guided reading text during the workshop, which enables them to practice their reading and build reading competence and stamina.

During **independent reading**, students silently read "just right" books they've selected on their own or texts from the guided-reading lesson. Independent reading is the perfect opportunity to increase the amount of time students spend reading. It also enables them to practice and expand reading strategies they've learned in read-alouds and shared and guided reading. Students keep an ongoing log of what they read so that over time they can evaluate the types of texts, genres, and authors they've read. They confer with the teacher and reflect on some of their reading in a journal.

LOW TEACHER SUPPORT

Using the Literacy Framework

As children move through the intermediate grades they encounter increasingly demanding expository texts. Expository texts present readers with challenges that are not often found in the narrative texts they're used to.

Michelle Zimmerman discovered during a social studies lesson that many of her sixth-grade students had difficulty reading and following the author's argument in a persuasive text they were studying. Since her students appeared to have little experience with this type of writing, Michelle decided it was important initially to provide the support and input her students needed to successfully read and think critically about argumentative texts by giving a shared reading lesson.

She found a short newspaper article on the pros and cons of wearing school uniforms. Michelle knew her sixth-grade students would have definite opinions on the topic and that the article would generate a fair amount of discussion. She made a copy of the article on a transparency to use on the overhead projector and gathered the students in the meeting area for the shared reading lesson. She read the enlarged text as the students followed along. Then Michelle reread the text and did a think-aloud to model how to identify the main ideas and supporting ideas in each paragraph. She underlined the main ideas with a green marker and the supporting details with blue to make them stand out.

Michelle and the students returned to the overhead transparency of the article on subsequent days to discuss words and language structures that are especially relevant to argumentative texts.

Michelle says, "By using a shared reading experience to introduce, demonstrate, and model the way I read and make sense of a written argument, I make visible for students what a reader does when engaging with this type of text—or for that matter, any type of text. It's important that I demonstrate and show them the processes involved in accessing and using the information from the text first before I expect them to try it out themselves. Moving right into guided reading or asking kids to read argumentative texts independently just doesn't provide the level of support and input they need from me initially to read that text successfully."

Michelle's recognition of her students' needs led her to consider which instructional approach would provide the right amount of support, and from there she was able to select a suitable text with which to teach her students. The learners in our classrooms direct us toward the best approach and the most suitable kinds of text that will help us teach them. The graphic on page 24 shows some possible areas of consideration when planning for reading instruction in a comprehensive literacy framework.

A Closer Comparison of Read-Alouds, Shared Reading, Guided Reading, and Independent Reading

The following comparison of read-alouds, shared reading, guided reading, and independent reading shows how these teaching approaches work within a comprehensive literacy framework.

Read-Aloud Reading To	Shared Reading Reading To/With	Guided Reading Reading With	Independent Reading Reading By
The teacher reads from a standard-size text so the print may not be visible to most students.	The teacher reads from an enlarged text so all students can see the text.	Every student has a copy of the same text selected by the teacher.	Students select just-right text or guided reading text. Just-right text selection may require some teacher guidance.
Students listen while the teacher, the more expert reader, reads from a wide variety of texts.	The teacher works with the whole class or a small group to read an enlarged text. Students follow along silently or read aloud with the teacher.	The teacher works with a small group of four to six students. Students silently and individually read a text carefully selected by the teacher.	Students silently read self-selected and/or guided reading texts individually each day for a large block of time during reading workshop.
The teacher sets the purpose based on the learners' needs.	The teacher sets a purpose based on the learners' needs. The enlarged text is selected to meet the learners' needs.	The teacher sets a purpose based on the learners' needs. The text is selected to meet the learners' needs.	Students and teacher set goals based on learners' needs. As goals are met, new goals are set.
The text may be more challenging than texts all or some students could read independently.	The enlarged text may be new or familiar. It may be more challenging than texts all or some students could read independently.	The text is usually new to students, at an instructional level, and provides both supports and challenges.	The self-selected text is at an easy or instructional level that enables the reader to practice skills and strategies already introduced.
The teacher may pause occasionally to think aloud or demonstrate for students how she applies a reading strategy or skill in a text. Discussion of the text, concepts, events, ideas, vocabulary, themes, or language structures may vary from a little to a lot and is always in the service of making meaning.	The teacher reads and stops at planned instructional points in the text to model for students how she applies a reading strategy or skill. The students may join in with the teacher's help to try out what has been modeled and/or discussed.	The teacher introduces the text, sets a purpose for reading, and supports students as needed when they silently read the text themselves. Discussion of the text follows the reading. Students and the teacher may return to the text to support the discussion and thinking.	The teacher confers with students on a regular basis; observes students' reading behaviors, attitudes, and habits; and tailors instruction to meet the needs of the individual learner.
The teacher reads a wide range of texts, both fiction and nonfiction.	The teacher uses Big Books and lifted texts on an overhead projector so all students can see and/or read the text. Selections include a wide range of fiction and nonfiction texts.	The teacher often selects short texts that students can read in a few sittings. Selections include both nonfiction and fiction texts.	Students read a wide range of both fiction and nonfiction texts. These may include novels, newspapers, poems, magazines, interviews, biographies, and plays.

Three Key Elements That Inform Instructional Decisions in a Comprehensive Literacy Framework

When planning for instruction, it is vital to consider the following three elements; each element informs and serves as a prerequisite for the next:

- The learners' needs
- The various instructional approaches available and the level of support each offers
- The types of texts—either fiction or nonfiction, in varied forms and genres—that will give students a wide range of reading experiences during instruction

The Learners' Needs

When planning your teaching, it's important to start by asking two questions about the learners' needs.

- What do students already know?
- What do they need to learn?

Students bring diverse backgrounds, experiences, interests, reading abilities, and literacy understandings to the classroom. Therefore, it's important to get to know each of your students as individuals. That's why ongoing assessment is so crucial (Chapter 2 discusses assessment at length). Having a good sense of what it is students need to know and what they already do know will help point you in the right direction when you're planning for instruction. Time is too valuable to be spent teaching students what they already know or what might be currently out of their reach.

Instructional Approaches

The various instructional approaches available, each offering a different level of support during instruction in a comprehensive literacy framework, enable you to meet the diverse needs of the readers in your classroom. For example, read-alouds and shared reading provide greater teacher support and input than independent reading, where students read on their own without any support. When you know your students well, you can make better decisions about how much support you need to offer them and which instructional approach—a read-aloud, shared or guided reading, literature study groups, partner reading, or independent reading—is best at any given moment.

Types of Text

Lastly, once you know your learners and which instructional approach you'll use to teach them, you have to consider what text to use to help get the teaching done. Often, when teachers plan, they *begin* with text selection and try to decide what to teach their students based on what that particular text has to offer. But it's far more effective to begin your planning with your learners' needs in mind. Once you know what students need to learn and which approach you'll use to teach it, then it's time to look for a suitable text that will help you meet your instructional goals.

Favorite Read-Aloud Books

Select fiction and nonfiction picture books instead of novels for some of your read-alouds. They are shorter in length and can often be read in one or a few sittings. Many books can be read in the period of time it would take to read one novel. Illustrations, photographs, and other graphics (visual elements such as diagrams, graphs, maps, and tables) in picture books offer students other avenues for understanding and information gathering. For students whose first language is not English, information and understanding generated beyond the words is one way to make texts accessible and provide an entry point into that particular text (Moline, 1995).

Here is a list of some favorite read-aloud books:

An Angel for Solomon Singer by Cynthia Rylant (Scholastic, 1996)

Chato's Kitchen by Gary Soto (Putnam, 1995)

Fox by Margaret Wilde (Allen & Unwin, 2000)

Freedom River by Doreen Rappaport (Hyperion, 2000)

Girl Wonder: A Baseball Story in Nine Innings by Deborah Hopkinson (Simon & Schuster, 2003)

I Wanna Iguana by Karen Kaufman Orloff (Putnam, 2004)

Ish by Peter H. Reynolds (Candlewick, 2004)

Kamishibai Man by Allen Say (Houghton, 2005)

Leonardo the Terrible Monster by Mo Willems (Hyperion, 2005)

The Librarian of Basra: A True Story from Iraq by Jeanette Winter (Harcourt, 2005)

The Man Who Walked Between the Towers by Mordicai Gerstein (Roaring Brook Press, 2003)

Mr. Peabody's Apples by Madonna (Callaway, 2003)

Show Way by Jacqueline Woodson (Putnam, 2005)

The Spider and the Fly by Mary Howitt, Tony DiTerlizzi (Simon & Schuster, 2002)

Through My Eyes by Ruby Bridges (Scholastic, 1999)

Train to Somewhere by Eve Bunting (Houghton, 2000)

Voices in the Park by Anthony Brown (DK, 2001)

Weslandia by Paul Fleischman (Candlewick, 2002)

Planning for Teaching: Consider the Learners' Needs, the Approach, and the Text

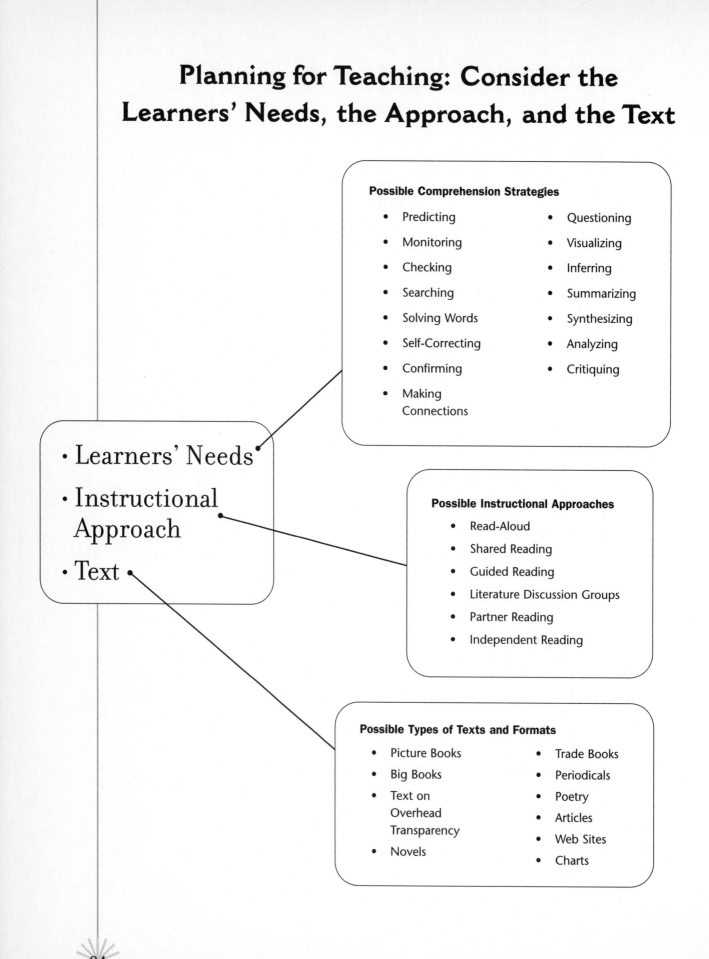

- Learners' Needs
- Instructional Approach
- Text

Possible Comprehension Strategies

- Predicting
- Monitoring
- Checking
- Searching
- Solving Words
- Self-Correcting
- Confirming
- Making Connections
- Questioning
- Visualizing
- Inferring
- Summarizing
- Synthesizing
- Analyzing
- Critiquing

Possible Instructional Approaches

- Read-Aloud
- Shared Reading
- Guided Reading
- Literature Discussion Groups
- Partner Reading
- Independent Reading

Possible Types of Texts and Formats

- Picture Books
- Big Books
- Text on Overhead Transparency
- Novels
- Trade Books
- Periodicals
- Poetry
- Articles
- Web Sites
- Charts

Final Thoughts

Guided reading is an instrumental component of a comprehensive literacy framework—one important step on the road to independent reading and writing. When you carry the thread of instruction across this framework—from read-alouds to shared reading to guided reading and then into independent reading—you help students envision the work you ultimately expect them to do on their own. It is important to make use of all approaches in all grade levels. For example, once students observe and share in the demonstration of a strategy, their grasp is further strengthened by actual performance. If instructional methods such as read-alouds and shared reading experiences were eliminated in the intermediate grades, students would miss out on essential opportunities for teacher demonstration and direct instruction, and this would adversely affect their practice and independent reading and writing. In addition, the threads that hold the framework together would be weakened and the different levels of teacher support that contribute to student learning would be lost.

Observing students as they engage in the various reading and writing experiences within the framework helps you determine what students are learning and what they need to learn next, providing you with valuable insights and direction regarding which instructional approach would be the best one to meet students' needs. Reflect on your reading workshop. Be mindful of the components or approaches you already make use of to support and energize your students as readers. Do your part to add the missing components that you need to strengthen and enhance students' thinking and learning so there is a balance of approaches you capitalize on in the course of a day, a week, and a month. Give careful attention to the planning and the delivery of your instruction so students learn more about being readers.

In the next chapter, I discuss assessment and the valuable information it can provide about the readers in your classrooms. I describe a variety of ongoing assessment tools that can help inform your reading instruction and plan your guided reading lessons. I share ways in which you can gather assessment information directly from students, making it a natural part of your daily teaching.

Chapter 2

Dana Moury uses individual reading conferences to learn more about each reader in her fourth-grade class. She tunes in to what the reader is saying and how she can be helpful. She takes short anecdotal notes to inform her teaching and assessment of the reader.

Assessing Students and Forming Guided Reading Groups

Assessment, which involves collecting information about or evidence of your students' learning, is a continual and integral part of quality teaching. In fact, teaching without continual assessment is akin to "teaching without the children."

—Irene C. Fountas and Gay Su Pinnell, *Guiding Readers and Writers Grades 3–6*

I recall attending a workshop in which J. David Cooper, literacy educator and author, posed this question to the audience of teachers: "If you want to know how well students read and write, what do you need to have them do?" The audience replied in unison, "Have them read and write." We gave a knowing laugh because we understood Cooper's point: Only by carefully observing individual students in the course of ongoing reading and writing can we get to know each reader and writer in our classroom.

When it comes to making guided reading work, assessment is crucial. Assessment provides information about what your students already can do and about the help they need in their literacy development. Assessment in reading begins with getting to know each reader personally by collecting, through a variety of methods, information about students' understandings, attitudes, interests, and previous learning experiences as readers. In order for you to know the readers you teach, you must observe and interact with them, often recording responses, reading behaviors, and strategies they use while they read. Assessment is a continuous process that relies heavily on observation of students engaged in reading materials they are already using during reading workshop. When you watch and talk to a reader at work—engaged in the task you are assessing—you capture information about that reader's pattern of growth and ongoing needs, which you, in turn, can use to inform your teaching and the types of guided reading groups you form for instruction. Assessment becomes, as Fountas and Pinnell note, "a continual and integral part of quality teaching."

Ongoing Assessment Builds a Profile of Each Reader

When you consistently use assessment tools throughout the year to document your observations of students' actions as readers, you are able to determine students' strengths and learning needs. Certain assessment tools will give you necessary information at the beginning of the school year, while others should be used at the midpoint or end of the year, and still others will be used on an ongoing basis, all year long. The information you collect supports your instruction in the following six key ways:

1. It helps you find out what students already know.

2. It alerts you to what students need to learn.

3. It informs your planning and directs your purpose and teaching focus.

4. It helps you select the reading approach to use (read-aloud or shared, guided, or independent reading).

5. It assists you in determining the best type of grouping for instruction—whole group, small group, or individual.

6. It helps you determine the materials that are best suited for your teaching.

Your job is to get to know the students in your classroom and to find out what they know and what they can do as readers. Through assessment and evaluation of the data you gather over time, you gain essential knowledge about a particular reader's progress. As you analyze, reflect on, and evaluate the assessment information, you're building a profile of that reader *at work*. You can use that profile to plan for your instruction of that reader in guided reading and other instructional settings as well. Then, as you teach and as you reflect on that teaching and on the reader's learning, you are receiving new and more current assessment information. The key to the assessment process is its cyclical and ongoing nature: You gather information, analyze, reflect, evaluate, develop a profile, and instruct. Student progress is then continually reviewed as part of an ongoing assessment, and you plan once more. On the next page is a graphic illustrating this cycle.

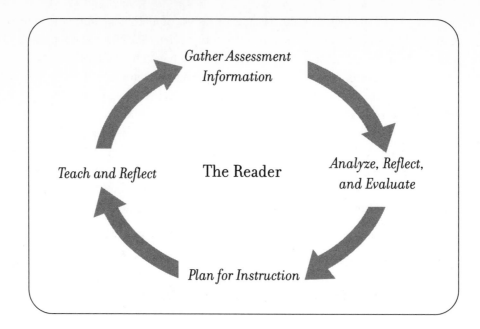

Gather Assessment Information

The Reader

Analyze, Reflect, and Evaluate

Plan for Instruction

Teach and Reflect

✳ Plan learning experiences and instruction.

What knowledge, skills, and strategies will students need to know to perform effectively? What learning opportunities or approaches will provide students with the knowledge, skills, and strategies? What will need to be taught and how will it be taught? What materials and resources should be used?

I use this process, as do many other teachers with whom I work. Here is one way you might try out the backward design process:

At the start of the year, begin by meeting as a grade-level team of teachers to talk about what you want to accomplish with the readers at your grade level. Start with a question such as What do we want our readers to know and be able to do by June? *Take a few minutes on your own to quickly list your responses. Then compile a chart of your team members' collective ideas. Next, discuss what is important for the students to be able to do, know, and demonstrate as readers. Lastly, talk about how you will collect acceptable evidence that shows whether students have met particular goals or objectives. As part of this entire process, take a close look at your state standards and district curriculum guides.*

Once you've determined the goals, formed a clear sense of the learning destination, and agreed on how you will substantiate what students have learned, create a typed list of your goals. Decide which ones you will focus on during the first several weeks of school. Assess your students so you have a clear idea of what they already know and can do. After four or five weeks, stop and take stock to figure out what students have learned. Make a list of where you will go next over the following several weeks. Keep a copy of the final draft of the list handy so that every few weeks you and your grade-level team can easily review the list to see how you're doing with getting the students to reach the goals you developed at the beginning of the year.

When we begin with the end in mind and have a clear destination, we know what it is students need to learn. Once the destination is clear, we can plan the various learning experiences, instructional approaches, and assessments to create the best road map to get there.

A group of fourth-grade teachers brainstormed this list describing what they want their students to be able to do as readers by the end of the school year. Here is the reorganized and typed version teachers kept handy for review.

Types of Assessment Information

When it comes to assessment, you have to decide *when*, *what*, and *how often*. You will need to plan time to assess students and devise a way to keep track of everything with well-thought-out assessment procedures. The types of assessments you use to gather information about students can take many forms. The assessments you choose should provide the information you need to develop the strategies and skills that will be the most beneficial to your students. Your evaluation of assessment information will help you plan for whole- and small-group instruction and individual conferences. In addition, the information you gather will help you determine how students should be grouped for guided reading.

Choose only the tools that work for your classroom and students, keeping in mind what it is you want your students to know and to be able to do as readers. It is important to assess at intervals and to use a variety of tools to get a complete picture of students' strengths and needs. In this section I discuss in detail seven assessment tools that I find particularly helpful. At the end of the section, I include a chart (pages 41–42) that sums up these as well as several other useful tools.

Individual Reading Conferences

Individual reading conferences provide the time and opportunity to observe and talk to students about their reading. At the start of the school year, use the conference time with every student to assess reading, discuss their experiences as a reader, identify some strategies and skills to focus on, and facilitate the self-selection of books that are best suited for independent reading. Think of individual reading conferences as repeated occasions to get a close-up view of how each student is doing. As you confer with students and get to know them better, you will have more assessment information at hand to assist in establishing guided reading groups. In addition, conferences offer the perfect opportunity to tailor your instruction to a student's specific needs, which may be difficult to address in a whole-group or small-group guided reading setting.

It's important to remember that classes of almost any size contain readers with varying needs. Don't get caught up in the idea that you have to give each student in your class equal conferring time; rather, think about giving students what they need to move forward as readers. The number of students you confer with during the reading workshop will depend on your observations and the needs of the students. Some conferences will be brief; you may simply be checking in to see how the reading work is coming along. Other conferences will run a bit longer; you may be teaching a specific strategy. But even in these cases, conferences should not run too long; short conferences keep your teaching focused. Think about your instructional purpose for a particular student and stick to it. If you try to teach too much, you will overwhelm students. Keep in mind that if both reading conferences and guided reading groups are a regular part of your reading workshop, other opportunities for teaching will be available to the students who need help.

One issue that can prove challenging is scheduling. How do you balance your individual reading conferences and your guided reading groups each week? Below is a graphic depicting how one sixth-grade teacher, Maddie Leon, manages to balance both kinds of groups over a two-week period. Notice how she schedules a week with guided reading groups on three days and individual reading conferences on the other two days, and then reverses this pattern the next week. On pages 32–33, you'll find a full description of how this teacher runs her reading conferences.

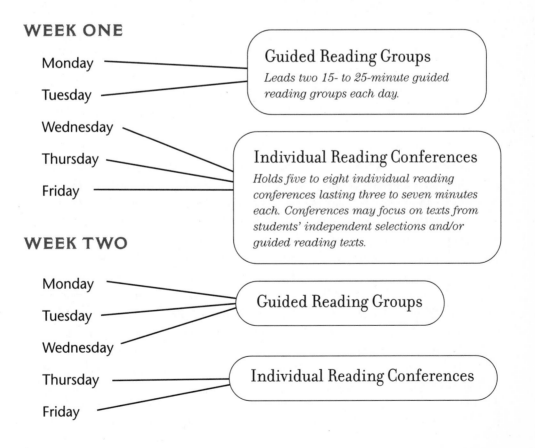

WEEK ONE

Monday

Tuesday

Guided Reading Groups
Leads two 15- to 25-minute guided reading groups each day.

Wednesday

Thursday

Friday

Individual Reading Conferences
Holds five to eight individual reading conferences lasting three to seven minutes each. Conferences may focus on texts from students' independent selections and/or guided reading texts.

WEEK TWO

Monday

Tuesday

Guided Reading Groups

Wednesday

Thursday

Individual Reading Conferences

Friday

The Reading Conference

During the first few weeks of school, Maddie Leon gathers assessment data on her sixth-grade students using various assessment tools. She holds baseline individual reading conferences with students to find out specific information about each reader. The individual reading conferences permit Maddie to interview each student about his or her reading experiences both in and out of school. She also uses the conferences to determine the appropriateness of each student's self-selected book choices. The conferences present the perfect opportunity to talk about what has happened in the book so far, to listen to the student read a short portion of the book aloud, and to talk about what he or she remembers from the reading. As Maddie observes the student reading, she jots down notes on the strategies and reading behaviors the student uses, which become part of her developing profile on that student.

Maddie explains, "Once a student has read a passage aloud, I always begin by talking about what was read. I want students to know that understanding and getting meaning out of what they read is the most important part of reading. But during the reading of the text, I also pay close attention to how the student problem-solves when he comes to difficulty. I record the oral reading behaviors I observe, noting if the student monitors for meaning and uses 'fix-up' strategies to quickly self-correct errors that interfere with the meaning. It's important that I have a clear sense of how each reader deals with the text when faced with some kind of difficulty. It's not just problem-solving the words, it could be understanding what they've read as well.

"I also take notice of how the oral reading sounds. I listen to see if the student is phrased and fluent. Fluent readers put groups of words together in natural, meaningful phrases, the way spoken language sounds. They also read with appropriate expression and attend to the punctuation.

"During individual reading conferences, I talk with students about what I observed and recorded in my anecdotal notes. I'm candid with students about what I've observed and about where their strengths lie, as well as where they need to focus their reading work. I often use the conference time for goal setting with students. Not only do the individual reading conferences help me get to know each reader in my class, they provide multiple opportunities in the first few weeks to listen to students read so I can tailor reading instruction to specific needs.

"In addition, I use the assessment data I collect to evaluate how I might initially group for guided reading. I look for common needs among students

(continued on next page)

and begin to form groups. For example, during individual reading conferences I noticed five students still having difficulty selecting just-right books for independent reading. Some of the students could read the words in the books they chose but didn't really understand what was happening. A few others were in books that were well beyond their instructional level. They had to consistently stop to problem-solve multiple words on each page. When I see students overworking their reading muscles to repeatedly figure out words, I know their processing systems are working too hard. How can you enjoy reading when you have to keep stopping to figure out yet another word? That's when I know I have to step in and do some teaching.

"I knew that even though their issues with selecting appropriate books were different, book choice was a general issue for all of them. When kids read independently, the texts they select should be read with relative ease. They should only have to problem-solve minimally as they read, and then they should be off again reading long stretches of text before they need to slow down to figure out another word. And, most important, they should be able to understand what it is they're reading. This is one of those groups that will stay together for a relatively short time—really just until they repeatedly experience what it feels like to be a reader in a 'just right' book and can choose appropriate books for themselves."

Sample record sheet for individual conferences. I use the form from Regie Routman's Reading Essentials *(2003).*

Sixth-grade teacher Jason Hardy records on a conference record sheet what he wants to remember about the reader and what he wants to help her with next. Together they set some goals. The students keep conference record sheets in their reading folder along with their reading log. That way, both the classroom teacher and resource teacher, who work in the classroom, can quickly review the last conference record sheet and the goals at the start of the next individual reading conference.

Anecdotal Records

Anecdotal records are a quick and easy way to record your observations of students as they engage in reading or discuss what they've read. Guided reading and individual reading conferences are perfect times to observe students in the process of reading and to document what you've observed. Develop a schedule of who will be observed each day, week, or month. Use a clipboard, notebook, or folder to record notes. It's best to use short phrases or quick notes for your observational comments, and remember to date the entries. Some teachers use abbreviations or a type of shorthand that makes it easy to quickly get their observations down and then later reconstruct their observations in greater detail.

Build a profile of the positive aspects you observe by focusing on what students *can* do. Pay attention to what students know and the range of skills and strategies they use as they read. You'll also want to look for persistent problems or issues and think about how and when you might help students with them during guided reading or individual reading conferences.

For example, the students in one of my guided reading groups were having difficulty problem-solving multisyllabic words in a particular text. I noted this and wrote down some of the words they had trouble figuring out. I used this information to plan some word-solving work near the end of the next guided reading lesson. My observations of the students during this two-minute word work helped me determine that the students needed additional practice, and I incorporated that practice into my instruction.

As you can see, anecdotal notes not only serve as a record of what the student is doing as a reader but also help direct the next instructional steps. Be sure to take sufficient time to analyze your records over time, looking for patterns and trends. The information you gather will help direct the instructional focus for individual reading conferences and for guided reading. In addition, what you learn can inform the student, parent, and other teachers who work with the student.

Anecdotal Record Sheet

Use with 3" x 3" Sticky-Notes

Sample of anecdotal records

> *A*necdotes about events in the reading/writing life of a student tell an ongoing story about how that child responds to the classroom's literacy environment and instruction. Since stories are how we make sense of much of our world, anecdotal records can be a vehicle for helping us make sense of what students do as readers and writers.
>
> —Lynn Rhodes and Sally Nathenson-Mejia, "Anecdotal Records: A Powerful Tool," *The Reading Teacher 45*(7)

Name	Informal Observations	Peer Interviews (do beginning of Oct.)	Baseline Conference	DRA	Standardized Tests	Other
Joseph	9/14 Self-selects Cross Creation; humor; some mystery to it too; on p. 24; held that central thought it sounded good.		S Comprehension Fast Reader W Choosing JRr books reading interview ✓	40 Makes good predictions and understands at literal level; partial understanding of important text points; quite a lot of details		Comedy - likes joke books fluent reader; phrased
Demitriyah	9/15 Self-selects The New Tattletale and the Horrible Truth; new movie wants to read book; likes fantasy; compare events/characters in both to movie (wants to do this)		S Visualization, Decoding Rereading W Skipping something returning choosing JR books reading interview ✓	70 High 6th; reads lots of fantasy; into Star Wars (wide reading); wants to try other genres (goal)		Book group or literature study group(?)
Jessica	2/13 Some difficulty finding a just-right book; read edition of Horrible Harry; phrased and fluent; problem relies on hand; made T→T connection		S Retelling W Decoding choosing JR books with help	28 Focused; rereads, monitors some. Some difficulty problem solving or rvw; able to retell characters, setting, events, & problem		Needs to wear reading glasses Writes words on paper to bring to room (unknown words) Fiction/Mystery (Reading buddy?)
Christofer	9/14 Self-selects Encyclopedia Brown takes the case; read Encyclopedia Brown before; like mysteries; can figure them out; pp 29 - likes chapter mystery; should I keep reading it & how?		Spanish S Self-questioning W Decoding words Comparing characters choosing just-right books reading interview	50 Reads large meaningful stretches of text; schools mostly fiction; good predictions; adequate summary in details & events		Fiction; likes playing soccer; outdoors fun
Yousef	9/13 Used the table of contents, to locate information and decide what to read in contests; reading text; captures main idea, able to tell about what his reading; uses text/self-selection		Ethiopian S Decoding fluency and W Comprehension choosing JR books	28 Reads fluently, but very limited comprehension even reading & discussing page at a time		Magazines Non-Fiction Sometimes skips things; Reading buddy(?)
Bo Hyun	9/15 Self-selects Freckle Monthly; unearth. Read last 3 days; able to tell gist of story so far		Korean Retelling good choosing JR books reading interview ✓	40 made several reasonable predictions; adequate summary with details; events, characters; good pace; monitors and self-corrects		Fiction; series books like Cam Jansen

Upper-grade teachers at Amy Dywer's school adapted the Student Data Chart from Still Learning to Read by Franki Sibberson and Karen Szymusiak. The chart provides a useful way to consolidate assessment information collected over the first few weeks of school. Analysis of the information provides teachers insight into the readers and writers in the class. It also helps teachers make decisions about small-group instruction for guided reading.

Reading Interviews and Surveys

Interviews and surveys help students think about themselves as readers and can provide you with many kinds of information and valuable insights, such as the students' overall attitudes about reading, the types of books they enjoy, the strategies they use, and what they think they need to improve to become better readers.

Interviews and surveys can be conducted orally or in writing and can be administered individually, in a small group, or in a whole-group setting. Keep interviews informal so students are at ease. You may ask the student to bring a self-selected book as a way to invite him to begin talking about himself as a reader. If the student responds in writing to the interview or survey, consider meeting with the student briefly afterward to discuss or clarify responses. Here are some topics and questions that can be discussed with the student or included in a written interview or survey:

Name: Diaia   Date: 9/14

Reading Interview

1. How would you describe yourself as a reader? A good reader because I like to read. If a book doesn't make sense I do different types of things to understand it — like reread or slow down. I think the more you read, the better you get.

2. What are you reading now at school? At home? How did you choose the book(s)? The Jumping Tree (at school). I just started it. I just finished Agnes Parker: Girl in Progress at home. I'm going to read Nancy Drew next. I've read others. I usually like novels. I usually read the book — front cover and the blurb on the back. Sometimes I read the first few pages before I pick a book.

3. What do you like to read (books, genres, authors)? Tell why. Mystery & novels of fantasy. I like reading of fantasy because you get to read about things that really aren't there and you can imagine your own things and how they would look in life. Roald Dahl is my favorite author. Most his books are fantasy. I've read Matilda, Charlie & the Chocolate Factory, and the Magic Finger probably.

4. What do you do when you can't read a word? I try to infer from words before and after. I try to break it down, see if there are words I know. I look for parts. Sometimes, I reread.

5. What do you do if you don't understand what you're reading? I try to reread it. If that doesn't help, I go back and break it down into small sections to try to understand just that part. Then I go on and read the next smaller part.

6. What kind of reading is easy for you? Hard for you? How do you know? Mystery because it's a type of book you put clues together and it's so easy for me to do. If you do, you infer. Kind of like putting a puzzle pieces together. A lot of the time when I get to the end & figured it out. Historical fiction is hard for me, because the words they use are words I'm not use to. Some of the words and phrases I don't know what they mean because of the time period.

7. What do you need to do to get better at reading? I'd probably need to try to see different points of view the author is making. Also, try to see if the author is telling me what is going to happen — give some clues — so you can figure out a twist to the story is coming.

8. How many books do you read in a week? In a month? Maybe a book every week or two; about four books each month.

- How would you describe yourself as a reader?
- What are you reading now at school? At home? How did you choose the book(s)?
- What do you like to read (books, genres, authors)? Tell why.
- What do you do when you can't read a word?

- What do you do if you don't understand what you're reading?
- What kind of reading is easy for you? Hard for you? How do you know?
- What do you need to do to get better at reading?
- How many books do you read in a week? In a month?

Record of Oral Reading

A record of oral reading is an informal assessment tool you can use to learn more about students' processing strategies by observing oral reading behavior. It is often called a modified miscue analysis or running record. During an individual reading conference, you sit next to a student and ask him or her to read a portion of a self-selected, just-right book. It may be a part of the text the student has already read or a part of the book he or she has yet to read. While the student reads, record observable reading behaviors such as substitutions, repetitions, self-corrections, omissions, insertions, and words appealed by the student or told by the teacher. It is also important to note the reader's pace, intonation, phrasing, and fluency.

Tania Dedham administers the Developmental Reading Assessment 4–8 (Beavers & Carter, 2003) to assess and document a fourth-grade reader's progress. The DRA is used as a baseline assessment with new students, midyear with students of concern, and at the end of the year with all students in grades 4–6.

TIPS AND TECHNIQUES

Benchmark Texts

Consider purchasing a commercial set of assessment or benchmark texts, such as the *Developmental Reading Assessment 4–8* (Beavers & Carter, 2003). The assessment texts are leveled for use in grades 4–8. Each grade-level set consists of two fiction and two nonfiction texts. The assessment consists of a student reading survey, oral and silent reading of a leveled text, and a written response to questions and prompts following the reading. This assessment works in conjunction with the *Developmental Reading Assessment K–3* (Beavers, 1997). The DRA is now offered in a second edition. The DRA2 includes fiction and nonfiction Benchmark Books in each kit for grades K–3 and 4–8, training DVD, and blackline masters on CD-ROM.

Following the reading, you may decide to teach on the spot what you've determined the student needs most. For example, if a student substituted a word that did not make sense and meaning was lost, and did not make an attempt to reread to clarify meaning and self-correct, you could use that error to teach the student what he or she could do in the future in a similar situation. You may also have the student retell what has happened or what was learned in the portion of the text read. If the text requires the student to do an inordinate amount of reading work, you and the student may select a more appropriate book together. For additional information on how to record students' oral reading behaviors, refer to *Miscue Analysis Made Easy* (Wilde, 2000) and *Guided Reading: Making It Work* (Schulman & Payne, 2000).

Retelling

An excellent way of checking on students' comprehension is to ask them to retell—orally or in writing—what they've just read. Retellings include key story elements or concepts from informational texts. Having students retell can give you insight into how well they've understood the text as well as the degree of control they have over oral and/or written language. During oral retellings, record students' statements telling what happened in a fictional text or what they learned from a nonfiction text. Sometimes it is necessary to prompt or ask questions. If the student gets stuck or omits information from the retelling, you may restate what he has told so far and say, "Tell me more" or "So then what happened?" or "What else did you learn?" Analyze both written and oral retellings for key points and elements, such as characters, important details, setting, vocabulary and special phrases from the text, events (noting whether they're in sequence or out of sequence), and the ending. Keep in mind that retelling can also be used to teach comprehension and can involve students in all modes of language—reading, writing, speaking, and listening. It requires students to recall, select, organize, and summarize information. Retelling can be varied to accommodate different levels of language ability. For example, ELL students' retelling procedures may include drawing to oral, and diagram to oral, and drama to oral and/or written.

Reading Log

A reading log is a type of journal in which students maintain an ongoing list of the books read throughout the school year. Reading logs help both student and teacher

Summary of Record of Oral Reading Conventions

Record what the child says on top and what the text says below. You may want to include the page number in case you want to go back to the text to do some teaching or to analyze the miscues at a later time. Some teachers record the type of error-meaning(M), structure(S), or visual (V) next to the miscue while the student is reading or later when analyzing the record of oral reading miscues.

Substitution	Child / Text	tried / tired
Omission	Child / Text	—— / tired
Insertion	Child / Text	very / —
Repetition	Child / Text	because|R
Self-correction	Child / Text	strange|SC / strict
Intervention	Child / Text	A / T

assess the amount, kind, and quality of reading over time. You may also use students' reading logs to form guided reading groups based on students' reading preferences and interests.

Define specific procedures for making entries in the reading log and demonstrate how to record information about the books students are reading. Use your own log entries or entries from another student's reading log as samples. You may find thinking aloud and demonstrating helpful when showing students how to record in their logs. Explain to students that, because they are copying the book or article title and the author's name, you expect correct spelling.

Consider having students review their reading logs quarterly to see what they notice about their own reading history. Students assume a larger role in their own progress when they take time to self-assess the amount, kind, and quality of reading they've done. Their involvement helps you and the students determine how well they are able to work independently and manage their own learning. (See Appendix, page 174, for a Quarterly Inventory of Reading.)

All upper-grade students keep a daily reading log. They review, analyze, and reflect on their reading quarterly. Some grade-level students complete a Quarterly Inventory of Reading form.

Reading List

Select a book to read. Enter the title and author on your reading list. When you have completed it, write the genre, and the date. If you abandoned it, write an (A) and the date you abandoned it in the date column. Note whether the book was easy (E), just right (JR) or a challenging (C) book for you.

#	Title	Author	Genre	Date Completed	E JR, C
11/30/06	You wouldn't want to be an Egytian Mummy	David Stewart	NF How-to	11/30/05	JR
12/4/05	Garfield chews the fat	Jim Davis	F Fantasy	12/4/05	JR
12/8/05	The Man who walked between the towers	Mordicai Gerstein	NF really happened	12/6/05	R
12/8/05	The Stranger	Chris Van Allsburg	F Fantasy	12/8/05	JR
12/14	The wonder of Light	Jan Adkins	NF Science	12/14/05	JR
13/14	Do stars have points?	Melvin and Gilda Berger	NF Science	A	JR
12/15	Poppleton has Fun	Cynthia Rylant	F Fantasy	12/15/05	E
12/15	The Usborne complete book of Magic	Cheryl Evans	NF Illusions	12/15/05	C
12/16	Abi yoyo	Pete Seeger	F Fantasy	12/16/05	E
12/16	The Illustrated book of Myths and Legends	Neil Philip	F Fantasy	12/22/05	R
12/16	The Illustrated book of Myths and Legends	Neil Philip	F Fantasy	12/22/05	R
12/16	The Illustrated book of Myths and legends	Neil Philip	F Fantasy	12/22/05	R
12/22/05	The Illustrated book of Myths and Legends	Neil Philip	F Fantasy	12/22/05	R

Reading Log

Title	Author	Date Completed	E, JR, H
Sélavi	Youme	3-27-06	JR
The Lotus Seed	Sherry Garland	3-28-06	JR
GOd	Daniel Kirk	3-28	JR
The True story of the Three little Pigs	Jon Scieszka	3-29-06	JR
PlantZilla	Jerdine Nolen	3-29-06	JR
My Home in Greece	Jenny Vaughan	3-29-06	JR
Abraham Lincoln	Wil Mara	3-30-06	JR
A. Lincoln and Me	Louise Borden	3-30-06	JR

Reading Response Journal

Reading response journals provide a dedicated place for students to chronicle their impressions, reactions, thoughts, and feelings about what they are reading. Response journals can be used before, during, or after reading. Students usually make an entry in the journal one or two times each week. A reading response journal serves a purpose for your students and for you. For your students, it's a place to capture their thoughts and voices, giving them a means to deepen their thinking and understanding as they reflect on their reading. For you, it's a tool to help you determine how well your students understand what they read by providing concrete evidence of what they see, feel, think, and remember as they read (Rosenblatt, 1978).

Response journals also provide a path to your conversations in guided reading groups or individual reading conferences about how the student experienced the text and made sense of what he read. Writing about what one reads requires reflection. When readers write about what they've read, it deepens their thinking about and understanding of what they read and reading in general.

Journal entries are usually open-ended and don't rely on sentence starters, which can narrow or inhibit students' responses. Since students record their thinking, the response journal is written in draft form. Students may be graded on the content, but they are not graded on spelling, punctuation, and handwriting as they would be if this were a formal assignment. Students frequently bring response journals to their guided reading groups and individual reading conferences so they can review, reflect on, and share their written responses. The conference discussions about the written responses also serve to expand and deepen students' understanding of the text.

You can introduce response journals by modeling journal entries with the whole group. Keep in mind that your demonstrations should resemble the ways in which real-world readers would respond. One way to ensure authenticity is to consider how you would respond to a friend after reading a book or going to a movie. What is it you'd want her to know about your reactions, thoughts, feelings, or discoveries? Here are a few ways students have responded to their reading.

- **React to the story line, what's going on in the book, or to the topic of a nonfiction text.**

  11/3—I just finished a bookmarked online article about volcanoes. They are so cool. I want to read more about Mt. St. Helens. I especially liked finding out about the eruption in May 1980. The article had great photos so you could see the before and after pictures of the mountain. The one I really liked showed how the volcano collapsed and caused a huge landslide. It covered 24 miles. Mt. St. Helens is showing signs of erupting again. I plan to read more about it.

- **Question or wonder about something.**

  2/7—I am reading Wringer *by Jerry Spinelli. It is the second book I've read by him. Right now I'm wondering if anyone will find out that Palmer is keeping a pigeon named Nipper as a pet. Also, what will Palmer do when he turns 10 and pigeon day comes? I know I could never wring a bird's neck. Gross!!!*

- **Make connections (to self, another text, or the world).**

  3/8—I was reading that about 1,000 twisters occur in the U.S. every year. Many of them happen in Texas, which is where my Uncle Tim lives. He told me he saw one once. He said it was so close you could feel it in the air. I heard on the news that if a tornado is sighted, it is called a tornado warning. I know twisters have awesome power. They can throw cars in the air, totally destroy houses, and pull trees right out of the ground.

TIPS AND TECHNIQUES

Ideas for Reading Response Journals

Let your students' active thinking and honest responses to texts help guide and determine the many possible reading responses. Here are 13 additional ways students might respond to their reading:

1. Predict what will happen from the title and/or blurb.

2. Predict what will happen next in the text.

3. Give an opinion. Explain your opinion.

4. Describe how the text is different from or the same as other books or texts you've read.

5. Create a nonlinguistic representation (visual picture) of your thinking about the book or text. Explain the meaning behind the image.

6. Consider why the author may have written the book or article.

7. Describe the research that might be necessary to write this book or article.

8. Share a favorite quote, sentence, or passage. Tell why it is a favorite.

9. List, describe, or sketch what you learned or new information that you obtained from the book or article. How does it fit with what you already knew?

10. Tell what made the text easy or difficult to read. Provide examples.

11. Explain how you dealt with unusual, difficult, or technical vocabulary.

12. Tell what you'd ask or say to the author.

13. Describe what you would say to encourage a friend to read the book or article.

Quick-Reference Chart of Selected Assessment Tools

Here is a list of assessment tools to consider when collecting systematic information on students' reading. It sums up the seven items discussed in the preceding section and includes a few additional tools. Collect only the assessment data that is truly useful, provides evidence of students' learning, and informs your teaching.

Assessment Tool	Description of Use	Suggestion for Frequency of Use
Anecdotal Notes	Write brief comments about observed behaviors for each student during reading and writing workshop, cooperative groups, and other content subjects. Focus on what the student can do.	All Year: Select a few students per day/week/month to observe and take notes on. Date each entry.
Audiotape Recordings	Make tape recordings of oral reading. Provide a tape for each student or ask students to bring one. Teach students to do the recording themselves.	Beginning/Middle/End of Year: Label and date entries.
Benchmark Books	Select books with a progression of difficulty to assess the different levels of readers within the classroom. Give students a brief introduction. Take a running record or note observations in a record of oral reading. Have students retell to determine if the level is appropriate. Use the information to assess the reading ability and to form a plan for guided reading groups. Commercial benchmark books such as the *Developmental Reading Assessment (DRA)* are available.	Beginning/End of Year: Use midyear as needed with select students.
Reading Interviews/Surveys	Use these to determine students' habits, attitudes, and understanding and awareness of the reading and writing processes.	Beginning of Year
Performance Samples in Reading and Writing	Have students choose a page from the book they are reading, a sample of writing they have completed, or a representative sample of a piece of writing that reflects the writing process: prewriting, draft, revision, editing, and final copy. Photocopy the selection. Have students write on a 3 X 5 card why they chose the sample and what they did well as readers/writers. Record responses for students who are unable to write their own. Model how to do this. Attach students' comments to performance samples.	Beginning/Middle/End of Year: Date samples and note changes.
Individual Reading Conferences	Meet with individual students to talk to them about their reading. The conference might include discussing book selection, talking about the storyline or topic, listening to the student read aloud a small portion, extending fix-up strategies, or setting goals.	Baseline; every 1-2 weeks meeting more often with struggling readers.
Record of Oral Reading	Use to record a student's oral reading. While the student reads the teacher records observable reading behaviors such as substitutions, repetitions, self-corrections, omissions, and words appealed by the student or told by the teacher. See the Appendix for a summary of standard coding conventions teachers use.	Baseline; Ongoing *(continued on next page)*

Reading and Writing Checklists	Checklists usually provide a list of expected observed behaviors or strategies that are part of students' learning. Some checklists can be completed by the teacher and others by students. Develop checklists with students to self-evaluate.	Beginning/Middle/End of Year
Reading Logs	Students maintain a daily record sheet of what they read. Decide what information is important to include. Model for students how to complete. Students can review logs and write a reflection and/or graph the time spent reading in school and at home. Note the kinds of books being selected and the kinds of writing being done.	All Year: Ongoing.
Reading Response Journals	Students respond in writing to something they have read or learned. Date all entries and establish clear criteria for what makes a good response. Periodically, select or have students select samples of their work. Review and analyze content of entry. Summarize the learning or reading. Reflect on the next instructional steps. These journals are drafts and serve as a place for thinking and learning. They may be graded for content but not mechanics.	All Year: Students write in reading response journals 1–2 times each week. Use other tools as necessary. Date entries.
Retelling	Students retell orally or in writing what they read. Retelling can be used after reading fiction or nonfiction. During oral retellings, jot down brief phrases and statements to capture students' words of what happened or what they learned from the text. Analyze both written and oral retellings for key points such as characters, important details, setting, vocabulary and special phrases from text, events in sequence or out of sequence, and ending. Prompt by saying "Tell me more" or ask questions to focus student on certain points or ideas in the text.	All Year: Ongoing or as needed after reading a text.
Rubrics www.tlt.ab.ca/ tlresources/rubrics_ new.html www.middleweb. com/rubricsHG.html	Scoring tool that lists the criteria for a piece of work. It provides specific standards or criteria the student must have to receive a certain score or rating. Use rubrics to assess different types of writing, retelling, projects, oral presentations, etc. Rubrics can assess the writing of individual students, the class, the grade level, and/or the school. Results provide specific information for teachers to make instructional decisions. Model for students how to self-assess their writing using a rubric.	All Year: Create and use as necessary.

Organizing, Storing, and Using Assessment Information

Establishing a manageable and useful data-storing system with opportunities to review and reflect on each student's ongoing learning is critical for making good decisions about what to teach and what instructional approach to use. Here are four ideas to organize and store assessment information:

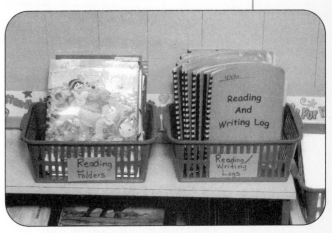

1. Keep current student assessments in a three-ring binder. Use dividers to create a section for each student. On a quarterly basis remove all but the latest assessment, placing the older ones in a student file folder. This method keeps the binder from getting too full and provides an opportunity to review and reflect on each student when filing the quarterly assessments.

E.J. Green's fifth-grade students store their reading and writing logs in baskets near the classroom library area.

2. Use crates, boxes, or file cabinets with vertical file folders. Some teachers provide students with two folders— a current assessment folder and a cumulative folder. The current folder stores the student's most recent assessment information. Each quarter remove and review all the assessment from the current folder and place in the cumulative folder.

Jason Hardy's students keep their reading folders in portable storage drawers alphabetized by the students' last names.

Jason Pannutti three-hole-punches a manila folder for each student and places it alphabetically in the binder. Anecdotal records and individual conference record sheets are kept in each student's folder in the binder. A student's individual folder with all their assessment information can be easily removed for conferring with the student and/or parent. Jason places the folders of students he plans to confer with in the front cover pocket. Blank conference forms are kept in the back cover pocket.

3. Purchase or request that students supply small spiral notebooks to record anecdotal notes during individual reading conferences. Some teachers record observations on sticky-notes or large address labels during guided reading and add them to students' spiral notebooks.

4. Use a status-of-the-class (Atwell, 1998) anecdotal form one or two times each week to get a quick snapshot of what all students will be doing during reading workshop that day. Write students' names ahead of time in alphabetical order on the status-of-the-class form. Make copies of the form with students' names already written on it and keep it on a clipboard for easy access to your information.

Using Assessment to Inform Instruction: Forming Guided Reading Groups

All types of small-group instruction are based on ongoing reading assessments of students. It's crucial to take the time to get to know your students by talking to them about their reading. Find out what they read, what they understand and learn from their reading, and how their reading relates to their personal experiences. Listen to them read portions of a text to gain a better understanding of their reading behaviors and strategies, especially at a point of difficulty in their reading. When you get to know each student in your classroom in this way, you will begin to see patterns of common needs emerge; from there you can consider grouping students in ways that will offer them the most beneficial reading instruction.

As I mentioned in Chapter 1, you can use guided reading in the intermediate grades for a variety of objectives. Form groups flexibly according to any of the following criteria: ability; specific need/focused task; reading strategies; or interest. Whichever criterion you use to form groups, the governing principle is the same: Students grouped together should share a common need and/or interest, which you will have determined through assessment. Let's take a look at how one teacher makes decisions about how to group students in his fourth-grade classroom.

Mr. Green's Needs Assessment
September

Name	Text Level	Needs
Brandy	20 Upper DRA	Processing texts to understand, fix-up strategies, reflection
Ken	28 Primary DRA	Monitoring, self correcting, fix-up strategies
Brianna	24 Primary DRA	Comprehension in general; reading for understanding
Oscar	28 Primary DRA	Fluency/phrasing, monitoring; fix-up strategies
Angie	34 Primary DRA	Book choice, inferring, summarizing
Kelly	34	Book choice, inferring, literal
Saad	38 Primary DRA	Book choice, context clues, inferring
Blanca	30?	Fluency/phrasing, context clues, literal, inferring
Jacelyn	40?	Inferring, summarizing, context clues
Alan	40	Inferring, reflection
Chris	40	Comprehension; phrasing/fluency; inferring
Keona	40	Pacing, Literal, Inferring
Nikko	40	Pacing, inferring, reflection
Sebastian	40	Literal, inferring, reflection
Chaliss	50	Summarizing
Katie	50	Inferring
Neha	50	Inferring, summarizing, reflection
John	50	Reflection, inferring, summarizing
Megan	60	Fluency/phrasing, inferring, reflection
Osmin	60	Inferring, summarizing

E.J. Green's Needs Assessment

How One Teacher Groups Students for Guided Reading

Dak Smith observes his students during reading workshop and other learning activities throughout the day. He groups students for different purposes depending on what he has noticed about them as readers. Of course, he cannot reach every student every day, so needs-based grouping gives his teaching maximum impact. Take a look at Dak's observations of his students and the grouping decisions he makes to best meet their instructional needs during reading workshop.

Ability

During a science lesson, Dak noticed that four struggling readers were not using illustrations, photographs, or captions when reading the text. Although Dak's science lesson demonstrated the importance of nonfiction features and involved student participation, Dak realized these four struggling readers needed additional practice reading nonfiction texts. Based on his observations, he determined that these students did not know that, as readers, it was important to pay attention to text features such as titles, headings, boldface print, italics, captions, and labels when reading. Dak grouped the four students for guided reading for a few weeks to help them learn how to use various nonfiction text features to navigate texts and gain salient information when reading. He began by selecting a short nonfiction text on tornadoes that included text features such as headings, photographs, illustrations, captions, charts, and maps and that all students would be able to read over several days. Discussions before and after reading focused on why the various text features are included and how they support the reader by guiding the way through the text, signaling what is to come, and helping to distinguish or separate important information from less important information. The students specifically looked at the illustrations, photographs, and captions to determine the purpose and nature of the features and how they help readers understand more about tornadoes.

Specific Need/Focused Task

After observing oral reading, Dak noted that five of his students never stopped to figure out the meaning of difficult vocabulary when reading. He decided to bring them together for a focused lesson on context clues to teach these students how to "read around" difficult words. Dak planned to show them how a reader can sometimes use the text that comes before or after the difficult word to figure out its meaning. He also planned to show the students that it's sometimes difficult to figure out the word from the text alone, so the reader needs to use information provided in the text to infer the meaning. Dak selected a short article that had

(continued on next page)

some unusual vocabulary, yet one that all five students would be able to read, applying the skills being demonstrated. After observing the students in the first lesson, Dak decided the students needed more practice. He chose additional texts that contained the same sort of challenges, thus focusing on specific needs of these students. The students were grouped together for three more guided reading lessons. Dak continued to observe them in guided reading and during individual reading conferences to determine if they were monitoring their reading and figuring out difficult vocabulary.

Reading Strategies

After a shared reading lesson on inferring, Dak realized that six students still seemed confused by what it means to infer when reading. He formed a guided reading group with these six students to help them practice using what they already know—what's in their head—together with the author's words to infer meaning. Dak selected a short series of cartoons with minimal text to give the students practice using context clues to understand more than was being explicitly stated. He chose cartoons initially because the spaces that separate each panel helped the students to understand that inferring is a matter of filling in the missing information by putting the clues together. After reading the cartoon on their own, Dak asked the students to infer the possible events that could come before, in between, and after each panel. The students used evidence from the text, pictures, and/or their own experiences to substantiate their inferences. Dak then moved from cartoons to short texts, which required the students to practice the strategy again. Not until Dak observed—in both guided reading and individual reading conferences—that these students had a better understanding of inferring did he consider regrouping the students.

Interest

After reviewing students' reading logs, Dak noticed that four of his students consistently chose only fantasy texts for independent reading. Because he wanted his students to try a variety of text types even during independent reading, he decided to group these students together for a short time to motivate them to read other types of material. He was aware that all four students were also interested in animals because each had told him so in the interview at the start of the school year. Therefore, Dak selected an excerpt from a longer nonfiction book about unusual animals for them to read during guided reading. If the students found the excerpt engaging, they would read the book. In addition, he used some time during guided reading to help the four students review their reading logs and set goals for trying out a new genre during independent reading to extend the types of texts they selected to read.

Dak explained, "Observing my students not only during guided reading and individual reading conferences but also across the day helps me determine what they know, what they can do, and what they still need to learn. I look for common needs and patterns, which help me decide how to form and reform groups for guided reading. By being flexible with grouping for guided reading, I can provide the most effective instruction readers need at the time."

When forming groups, think about your instructional purposes and how to meet them while responding to students' needs. You should have a clear sense of what your learners' needs are through your evaluations of a variety of assessments: reading interviews, reading conferences, book discussions, reading logs, observations, and anecdotal notes. In addition, you should observe students during writing workshop, as well as in other subject areas.

Remember that these groups are fluid and flexible. Some groups will form and disband in a relatively short period of time, perhaps only a couple of meetings. Other groups will have more longevity. Maintain each guided reading group as long as the need dictates. And remember to be responsive to each student in a group, keeping in mind that readers develop at different rates. Change groups when appropriate as you identify the instructional needs of individual students.

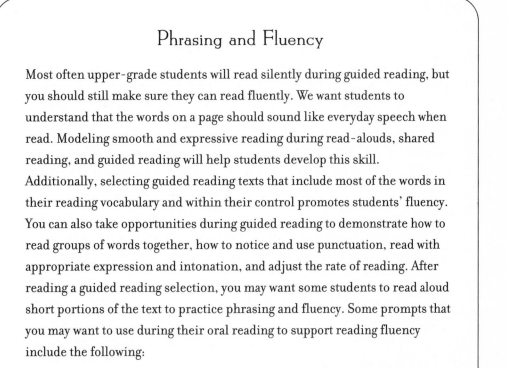

E.J. Green's list of students' instructional needs based on DRA text-level information and observations of students' reading during reading workshop

---

Phrasing and Fluency

Most often upper-grade students will read silently during guided reading, but you should still make sure they can read fluently. We want students to understand that the words on a page should sound like everyday speech when read. Modeling smooth and expressive reading during read-alouds, shared reading, and guided reading will help students develop this skill. Additionally, selecting guided reading texts that include most of the words in their reading vocabulary and within their control promotes students' fluency. You can also take opportunities during guided reading to demonstrate how to read groups of words together, how to notice and use punctuation, read with appropriate expression and intonation, and adjust the rate of reading. After reading a guided reading selection, you may want some students to read aloud short portions of the text to practice phrasing and fluency. Some prompts that you may want to use during their oral reading to support reading fluency include the following:

(continued on next page)

- Read it so it sounds like you're talking.

- Read groups of words like this (model phrase units).

- Read this part all together (cover part of print to show the phrase unit).

- Read it like the character is talking.

- Read the punctuation.

- Briefly pause when you see a comma (dash or ellipsis).

- Read it the way you think the author wants that part read.

Final Thoughts

Think of assessment as a continuous process of observing and interacting with students, often recording responses, reading behaviors, and the strategies students use while they're engaged in reading. These observations are what drive your future teaching decisions.

Make sure the assessment tools you use provide valuable information about individual students as *readers*. Otherwise, you're wasting your time, and the students' as well. Take stock of whether the assessment tool you're using is collecting enough useful information. Remember, the assessment information you gather, analyze, and reflect upon needs to enhance your teaching of reading, so your students can make real gains and move toward reading competency.

In the next chapter, I describe a framework for planning and teaching a guided reading lesson. It includes how to set a purpose for reading, choosing the text, helping students tune in to the text before reading, reading the text, and returning to the focus and digging deeper to extend thinking and learning after reading.

Chapter 3

Keith Matias meets with a group of fourth graders for guided reading. He provides a brief, focused introduction before reading to engage students in some discussion and help them tune in to the text.

A Practical Framework for Planning and Teaching Guided Reading Lessons

If children struggle with too many challenges, comprehension and enjoyment become compromised. We need to keep in mind that a guided reading session is about setting the group up for success.

—Tony Stead, "Comprehending Nonfiction: Using Guided Reading to Deepen Understanding," from *Spotlight on Comprehension*

Guided reading allows you to monitor students' reading development, assess what they need, and guide them as they learn to deepen and strengthen their understanding as readers of a variety of texts. When you meet with small groups in guided reading sessions, you can build on what your students already know as independent readers.

The Critical Role of Guided Reading Within the Learning Continuum

Recall from our discussion in Chapter 1 the learning continuum, with its gradual release of responsibility for learning to learners themselves. Along that continuum, guided reading lessons hold a unique and pivotal place. According to developmental psychologist Lev S. Vygotsky, learning is easier for children when they have the following:

❋ opportunities to participate in literacy activities that are consciously guided by a more expert other who understands how to do something and assists them in doing it

❋ support from a more expert other who knows the child well enough to have a clear understanding of what he or she needs to learn next

❋ opportunities to actively play a part in their own learning

In essence Vygotsky suggests that a child can do with help what he cannot yet do alone. Vygotsky refers to this as working in the learner's *zone of proximal development* (ZPD), where students can learn and complete a task with the teacher's support that they cannot yet do all by themselves. When teachers work in a student's ZPD, they provide the assistance and instructional support he needs to be successful with a task. If teachers give a student a task outside her ZPD, it will be too hard and create frustration no matter how much support is given. For example, expecting a student who's reading two years below grade level to read and comprehend grade-level texts will likely result in frustration and failure no matter how much support is given. Similarly, when teachers give a student a task in the *zone of actual development* (ZAD), where the student already can do the task independently, there is little new learning, though such tasks may build confidence and fluency. Through repetition and the gradual release of the task from the teacher to the learner, what was once in a student's ZPD moves into the ZAD. Jeffrey Wilhelm (2001) refers to this experience with the support of another as a learning-centered teaching process and represents it as follows.

1	2	3	4
I DO	I DO	YOU DO	YOU DO
YOU WATCH	*YOU HELP*	*I HELP*	*I WATCH*

Guided reading fits into Vygotsky's concept of the learning zones and the learning-centered teaching process. When you carefully select and introduce a text to students before reading, briefly interact with them and support them during reading, and extend their thinking and understanding after reading, you make it possible for students to learn more than what they could on their own. Guided reading allows you to teach at the cutting edge of readers' understanding and learning.

Planning the Lesson: A Step-by-Step Guide

In this chapter, I share a framework for planning and teaching guided reading lessons. The framework includes the following elements:

- **Set a focus for the lesson.** What do the students need to learn based on ongoing observation and assessment?

- **Choose the text.** What text will provide a high degree of support and manageable challenges?

- *Before* **reading: Tune in to the text.** What is the best way to introduce the text so students can access their background knowledge, engage in some discussion, and prepare for the reading?

- *During* **reading: Students read the text.** What are the students' and teacher's role during reading?

- *After* **reading: Return to the focus and dig deeper.** How will conversation and discussion support and extend the focus for reading and fuller understanding?

Set a Focus for the Lesson

Deciding ahead of time the focus for the lesson is critical to keeping the lesson short, teaching what the students need, and not teaching too much. When I determine what to teach, I consider just what will move a particular group of students forward as readers. I think about the students' specific learning needs as a result of ongoing observations and assessment information gathered during read-alouds, shared reading, independent reading, and other contexts. Most important, I have in mind the comprehension strategies and skills students need to practice based on previous guided reading instruction.

Choose the Text

Choosing the right text is very important. The selected text must be at the group's instructional level. Instructional-leveled texts are those that provide students with substantial supports and only a few challenges (Fountas & Pinnell, 2001b). There are a minimum number of new concepts, strategies, and skills necessary for the students to grapple with when reading. If the text has too many challenges, students may be prevented from problem solving while reading and may fail to grasp more than the surface meaning of the text. My aim is to choose a text that the students can read successfully with minimal help, but at the same time includes a sufficient number of challenges to stretch them a little.

While you can think about grouping and planning for guided reading in more flexible ways in the intermediate grades, it's still important to choose texts that match the level of the readers in any of the groups you form. When you place students with texts that are too hard, they spend most of their time struggling simply to get through the reading. The selection of a text and the type of small-group instructional focus and the purpose for reading you provide in guided reading need to support readers as they practice and apply what they've learned about being a strategic reader of texts. Here are 15 key questions to think about when selecting a text for guided reading:

1. What does this particular group need to learn now/next?

2. Can students relate to concepts or experiences in the text?

3. What background knowledge is necessary to understand the text?

4. What do I need to do to make connections between the text and students' experiences, previous reading, and/or the world?

5. Are there any texts from read-alouds, shared reading, or students' independent reading that will provide good connections?

6. What are the demands on the reader from this particular text?

7. Are there any surprising features about the layout and organization of the text?

8. What does the author want the reader to think or consider?

9. Are there any prominent aspects of the text structure such as problem and solution, cause and effect, or compare and contrast?

10. Is there difficult, unusual, or content-specific vocabulary that might present a problem?

11. Are there unusual print fonts?

12. Are there visual graphics—such as diagrams, charts, or maps—that require explanation or discussion?

13. What will I do to bring about genuine talk to arrive at greater meaning and understanding *before*, possibly *during*, and *after* reading the text?

14. What small-group, paired, or individual work will extend students' thinking and understanding of this text?

15. What would be a good follow-up topic or text?

Distinguishing Between the Focus for the Lesson and Purpose for Reading

When selecting the text and planning for a guided reading lesson, I think about both the *focus* for the lesson and the *purpose* for reading. I want to make a distinction between the two, because I view them differently. The focus for the lesson is the strategic action—questioning, inferring, summarizing, and so on—I've determined students need to practice to become more effective readers. The purpose for reading refers specifically to what students will read to find out or learn in that particular text, and often relates directly back to the focus of the lesson. For example, the focus of the lesson with one guided reading group was inferring. I selected a text that would support the focus for instruction and provided a brief introduction. Before the students began reading, I specifically stated the following purpose for reading: *Read to find out what kind of character Anthony is. Pay attention to what he says and does as you read so you can describe him, and also so you can support your thinking and reasons during our discussion after reading.* The instructional focus for this guided reading group most likely will stay the same over multiple lessons; what changes will be the purpose for reading the text on that particular day.

Before Reading: Tune In to the Text

Once you've selected a text based on a particular focus, introduce it to the students in the guided reading group. I often prepare students before reading through discussion, previewing the text, and relating personal experiences and ideas to the content. Use of read-aloud picture books, artifacts, videos, CD-ROMs, shared field trips, and graphic organizers are other ways to frontload information prior to reading and can even extend into discussions students have during and after they read.

Tuning in to the text at the beginning of the lesson gives you a chance to observe and support the students' thinking and ideas *before* they read. I react and respond to students the way I want them to respond to one another. As we tune in to the text selection, we lay out our thinking ahead of time, without fear of being right or wrong. Discussion before reading is vital because it supports understanding of the text. Below are some of the points we may target before reading when we are "tuning in."

- **Read and talk about the title of the text.**
  "The name of this article is 'Holding Back the Waters.' What do you think that title means? How could you 'hold back' water? What kind of article do you think this will be?"

- **Discuss what is already known about the topic and how that will influence the reading.**
  "What do you already know about volcanoes from our study and science experiment? How will that information help you as you read? What information do you expect to find in this article?"

> The more we frontload students' knowledge of a text or topic, the more we help them become actively involved in constructing meaning prior to reading, and the more likely they are to be engaged as they read the text.
>
> —Kylene Beers, *When Kids Can't Read: What Teachers Can Do*

- **Check out the cover and read the blurb on the back of the book to make predictions about the text or topic.**
  "The title of this book is The Big Five *by Keith Pigdon and Marilyn Woolley. Can you already tell what the big five are by just looking at the cover? Read the blurb on the back and see what else you can find out about these five animals and why the authors chose these particular animals to write about."*

- **Determine the type of text it is and discuss any clues about how the author will present the information.**
  "If the name of this book is Let's Graph It! *[by Elizabeth Kernan], what kind of book do you think this is? What makes you think that? What kinds of things do you think the author will include in the book? What makes you think that?"*

- **Predict and/or investigate the text features and/or graphics that may be included in the text.**
  "Where in the book can we look to see if the author includes different kinds of graphs? Look and find what other text features the author uses to organize the information for the reader."

- **Discuss any unusual, difficult, or technical vocabulary.**

  "There's one word I'd like you to look at in the table of contents. It's the title for Part 12, which starts on page 39. Does anyone know that word? Well, how do you think we would say it? I'll write it on the whiteboard so we can look at the parts and give it a try."

- **Discuss how the form of the text will help with reading it and/or how the form of the text will influence the pace of the reading.**

  "Why do you think the author used numbers in this part of the article? How will the ordering help you as a reader?"

- **Skim and scan the text to gather information by reading headings, subheadings, captions, and graphics.**

  "Quickly skim this article. What information can you get from just looking at the headings and graphics?"

- **Generate questions raised in the readers' minds by previewing the text.**

  "Let's jot down some of the things you're wondering about now that you've had a chance to preview the book."

- **Discuss strategies you want readers to use, especially if they have been a focus of your ongoing instruction.**

  "How might you keep track of the story events in this folktale as you read? One way is to try to picture what's happening. Run a movie through your mind as you're reading. We've been talking about how readers create mind-pictures when they're reading to help them remember and keep track of the characters and the events in the story."

- **Determine the purpose for reading the text.**

  "Today when you're reading I want you to pay close attention to the clues that help you know the main character is scared. What does she do and say that helps the reader know how she feels?"

During Reading: Students Read the Text

After I introduce the text and support the students' thinking before reading, students in the group each read their own copy of the text. It's important to make sure each student has an opportunity to read the entire text selection. Guided reading is not round-robin reading where each child in the group takes a turn reading. As the students read, they can mark, code, and record their thinking on the text with sticky-notes.

I may circulate and listen to one or two students quietly read aloud a short passage, providing support or reinforcement of the reading process and strategic actions. I jot my observations of errors and self-corrections as students read. I pay attention to what they do when they come to a difficulty. I listen to how a student's oral reading sounds—whether it is phrased and fluent or word-by-word and choppy. I use the on-the-spot information I gather to talk to and teach the reader. During the reading, I may focus on the following points:

- **Discuss the information the reader gathers from the text.**

  "What do you know from the part that you just read? How did you figure that out from what the author wrote?"

- **Inquire what is new information and confirm what the reader already knew.**

  "How do you know the mother's feelings toward her two sons changed? What do you know now about how the mother feels that you didn't know before?"

- **Discuss the most useful or interesting information read so far.**

  "What new or interesting information have you learned about Paul Revere? Why do you find that interesting?"

- **Clarify confusing or difficult parts of the text or unusual or technical vocabulary.**

  "You just read, 'The giant slept on a bed of withies, a mattress of twigs.' So, what are you picturing or thinking based on what you just read? How does the author help the reader understand the word withies?*"*

- **Discuss pace, phrasing, and fluency of the reading.**

  "Reread this part again where the character is talking, and this time make it sound like her. Try to slide the words together the way she would say them to her friend. When you read you want to read groups of words together so it sounds smooth—almost like someone is talking."

- **Discuss interpretation of graphic elements.**

  "What can we tell from the graph of 'How Much Sleep Kids Need vs. How Much Kids Get'? About how many hours of sleep do fifth graders need at night?"

- **Encourage the use of fix-up strategies for comprehension and/or difficult or unfamiliar words.**

  "You read [word]. Check to make sure what you read makes sense. Does it? How did that help you?"

- **Prompt for use of strategic action to problem-solve while reading.**

  "Do you know the first part of that word? Okay, now reread from the beginning of the sentence and think about what word would make sense in the story."

- **Talk about types of words that cause the most problems.**

  "Some of the longer words seem tricky for you. Let's try this one. Look at the parts. Try the first part. Now, say the next part. Can you say more?"

> *Taking turns to read a text is grossly uneconomical in that only one child gets to read at a time and it shifts the focus to accuracy at the expense of understanding.*
>
> —Don Holdaway,
> *The Foundations of Literacy*

As teachers we want to develop confident, competent, and discriminating readers who actively think and monitor their thinking as they read. Students need to know when they really understand what they're reading and when meaning breaks down and results in confusion. They also have to be flexible enough to know what possible ways they can repair what has caused the confusion.

After Reading: Return to the Focus and Dig Deeper

An important time to provoke thought—to take readers to a new depth of understanding—is *after* they've read. That is the time to "dig deeper" into the meaning of the text and to make connections beyond the text itself. It's important that students view the after-reading discussion as a conversation, where ideas are exchanged and explored. You may wish to start with a purpose-setting question or two to get the conversation started; similarly, a well-posed question can lift a conversation that's beginning to lose its momentum. However, the postreading discussion is not meant to be a question-and-answer session. Rather, this is a time to motivate thought, help make the text accessible, and facilitate a fuller understanding.

The length of the discussion after reading will vary depending on the purpose for reading, the amount of text to be discussed, and the level of understanding, engagement, and interest. Most discussions last 8–10 minutes.

Keep in mind, discussion is an integral part of the lesson before and sometimes during silent reading as well. Frequent discussion ensures students will understand the text and gives you lots of opportunity to model and practice strategies. Discussion encourages reflection on the strategies that have been used to help construct meaning and the ways in which information can be supported by finding evidence in the text. In addition, discussions during guided reading provide students with repeated opportunities to share their thinking, listen to others, consider different sides or perspectives, raise questions, examine a critical concept or topic from different angles, and make connections to their own lives, their reading, and the world. After reading, our discussions may focus on some of the following:

- **Interpret and respond to the meaning of the text.**
  "What does this text remind you of from your own life? What feelings do you have in response to the text?"

- **Locate, reread, and talk about the most important, interesting, or useful pieces of information.**
  "Which part(s) did you find most interesting? If you had to choose the most important point or idea in the text, what would it be? Why?"

- **Revisit the text to provide evidence of ideas and understandings discussed.**
  "Can you find in the text where we know for sure The Great One really likes The Pain? What words really convinced you? Does everyone agree? Why? Why not?"

- **Discuss prereading questions that were answered or unanswered, and new questions that have been raised.**
  "Let's go back to the questions we had before reading. Which ones were answered in our reading? Find where they were answered in the book. Which questions require more research or reading to answer? Do you have any new questions that came out of your reading? What else are you wondering?"

- **Locate, reread, and talk about sections that caused confusion or required clarification or deeper understanding.**

"Did any parts confuse you? Find a part that did and reread it. What about that seems to be confusing you?"

- **Problem-solve or clarify unusual, technical, or difficult vocabulary.**

  "Let's look at the tricky words that you all wrote on your sticky-notes while reading. Are any of them the same? Let's start with those. Find the first one in the text and read that part. Does anyone have an idea what that word means from what you just read? How do you know that—what did you read that helped you figure that out?"

- **Discuss use of reading strategies.**

  "Before sharing with the group, turn to your elbow partner and share the words or phrases you used to summarize each paragraph in the article. Make sure you tell him or her why you chose those words."

- **Discuss the author's purpose and whether sufficient information was provided.**

  "Why do you think the author wrote this article? What did she want the reader to learn about eating the right kinds of food? Do you think she provided enough convincing information? Why? Why not?"

- **Share a favorite passage or sentence.**

  "Take a minute to find your very favorite part in the book. Share that part with your elbow partner. Make sure you tell him or her why it's your favorite. Then we'll compare our favorite parts and reasons for choosing them with the group."

- **Interpret visual graphics such as charts, maps, and diagrams.**

  "Look at the Fujita Tornado Intensity Scale chart in the book. What information can we gather just from reading the chart? Why do you think the author included the chart for the reader?"

- **Analyze the features and/or discuss whether the format suits the topic and purpose of the text.**

  "How do you think the photographs and captions help the reader to understand more about the topic of Antarctica? Do you think they're important? Find a place where the use of photographs and captions adds to our understanding."

- **Discuss how else the story/information could have been presented.**

  "Can you think of another order or better order of events for this story? Why do you think that might be better?"

- **Discuss the accuracy of the information and any evidence of bias.**

  "Whose perspectives are heard in the book/story? Are there any perspectives missing? Who didn't get to tell their side?"

- **Determine if additional reading is desired or needed on the topic or by the author.**

  "You seem really interested in this topic and have additional questions. Let's check on the Internet to see if we can find some places we can book-mark to do some further reading. Maybe some of you can go to the library later this morning to see what other books there are on the topic."

Planning and Teaching the Guided Reading Lesson

Below is a comprehensive chart showing the four phases of planning and instruction for your guided reading lessons. This chart summarizes much of the information presented in the preceding sections.

Teacher Prepares for the Lesson	Before Reading: Tune In to the Text	During Reading: Students Read the Text	After Reading: Return to the Focus and Dig Deeper
• Decides where to meet with the guided reading group and makes available necessary materials. • Determines a focus, strategy, or skill based on students' needs. • Selects a text that provides support and manageable challenges. • Chooses a purpose for the reading. • Previews the text to plan the introduction, reading, and discussion. • Determines how to support and scaffold students before, during, and after reading. • Decides if text will be read straight through or chunked in a few portions to improve comprehension. • Plans for further reading or follow-up activities.	Teacher provides brief, focused introduction to the text. Teaching includes some of the following: • Explores what students already know about the topic. • Makes links to the knowledge and/or experiences students already have to the text content. • Probes students' responses during discussion. • Discusses selected text features, layout, unusual language structures, and/or unfamiliar vocabulary. • Uses anticipatory tasks such as previewing, skimming, and anticipation guides. • States explicitly the particular focus (strategy or skill) students will be practicing. • Sets a purpose for reading. • Provides for early finishers.	Teacher provides support while students read the text independently and silently. Teaching includes some of the following: • Decides if text will be read straight through or chunked in a few portions to improve comprehension. • Observes students' reading behaviors. • Checks use of strategies and comprehension by sometimes having students softly read a small section aloud to the teacher. • Makes a teaching point as needed with individual students. • Invites students to share their thinking. • Talks briefly with individual students about the text to clarify meaning and help with understanding. • Records observations to use for planning future lessons.	Teacher and students discuss the text to deepen their understanding of it. Teaching includes some of the following: • Maintains focus for lesson. • Returns to the purpose for reading. • Encourages genuine conversation and discussion. • Promotes listening to one another and talking about the text. • Probes students' responses during discussion. • Encourages students' questions and responses to one another. • Coaxes students to explain and justify thinking, comments, or points of view to one another by referring to the text. • Explores and makes explicit strategies students used to understand the text. • Explores concepts, vocabulary, and text features in greater detail. May use a whiteboard or chart. • Summarizes learning and focus. • Gives direction for further reading and/or next steps.

A Look at How One Teacher Plans for and Teaches a Guided Reading Lesson

Shele Banford noticed five students in her third-grade class who seemed to be having difficulty keeping track of events and clues in easy mystery chapter books during independent reading. After a bit of observation, Shele realized that the students were stymied by the gaps in the events or clues in the story. They weren't using and connecting information to fill those gaps. Since the students were experiencing similar needs, she decided to put them together in a small group for guided reading instruction.

Shele selected an easy mystery chapter book she knew all the students would be able to read with her support. The book she selected had both overt clues and some that required the reader to put the clues, or "puzzle pieces," together in order to fill the inference gaps. She met with these students almost every day over an eight-day period to guide and scaffold their thinking as they read the book. She focused on ways not only to keep track of the characters and story events but also to piece the multiple clues together.

Over the course of their reading, students began to notice the author had purposely left out pieces of the puzzle so readers could fill in some of the missing information themselves. As readers, they had to do more than simply rely on the overt clues in the text. In order to solve the mystery along with the story's detective, they had to make inferences based on the revealed events and clues gathered from reading to fill in the gaps along the way. Shele and the students talked about how mysteries worked and that it was important for readers to notice the way events and clues build to a climax before the mystery is solved.

Shele usually met with the group for about 15 to 20 minutes at the beginning of the reading workshop so the students would have the last 20 to 25 minutes to read the next agreed-upon portion of the text before the following meeting. She observed the students during both guided reading and individual conferences and decided the students would benefit from reading and discussing another similar mystery book. As the students read the second mystery, Shele found they required a little less support and scaffolding while reading.

Shele says, "When reading mysteries, students need to be critical readers. They need to have a sense of cause and effect and be able to assess vital information and facts as the story unfolds. I noticed as students moved into reading a second mystery book during guided reading that they were doing a better job of paying attention to the puzzle pieces laid out by the author. They were better able to define the story's problem and look for clues or evidence as they read. They were also better able to assess the evidence, connect the pieces of information to make inferences, and pretty much figure out a solution right along with the central character—the kid detective in this particular story.

(continued on next page)

"Discussions included more events and clues in the order they'd happened in the story. The students talked about how the actions of the characters built on the ones that came before and described how they put multiple clues together to figure out what might happen next. In fact, they would go back into the text to check, confirm, or substantiate their ideas and thinking during our discussions. We talked about how the story built and how the author picked up the pace to add to the excitement to purposely pull us along as readers to make us keep turning the pages to read more. I think most important, the students realized that in mysteries the reader is often figuring out the mystery along with the detective and that they have to notice the gaps in the story and make inferences to fill the gaps when reading.

"Grouping these students together for a particular purpose really made a difference. I think by reading, discussing, and charting basic characteristics of mysteries, the students have a broader and better understanding of the mystery story format and some of the devices authors use in this type of text or genre."

The following detailed chart shows Shele's initial thinking and planning for the lesson as well as the teaching decisions she made during the first guided reading lesson with this group of students. Shele divided the reading into two parts during the first lesson, stopping to talk to the students after they read the first six pages. When they were done discussing what they had read, students finished reading the remaining six pages on their own. Shele planned to meet with the guided reading group again the next day.

Plans and Preparations for the Guided Reading Lesson

Group: Michael, Tulia, Hannah, Dylan, Edward

During individual reading conferences, observations revealed similar needs and sources of confusion while reading self-selected independent mystery books; students are experiencing difficulty in keeping track of characters, events, and clues and in making inferences from the clues.

Text Selection
- Short, easy mystery book with some picture support, *Cam Jansen and the Chocolate Fudge Mystery* by David Adler
- Read with group regularly over 6–8 days

Materials
- Book for each student
- Chart paper
- Whiteboard and markers
- Sticky-notes for noting or flagging clues while reading
- Bookmark for marking place and recording pages to be read

(continued on next page)

Focus for Lesson

- Recognizing and keeping track of characters, events, and clues in longer texts
- Filling in inference gaps by connecting information presented in the text
- Recognizing and distinguishing some characteristics or features of mystery, which is a subgenre of narrative fiction (the mystery or crime to be solved, central character/detective, suspects, motives for committing crime, facts or clues, red herrings, etc.)

Preview Text

- Divide reading into portions (pages 1–6 and 7–12)
- Plan initial book introduction

DAY ONE

Before Reading: Tune In to the Text (approximately 5–7 minutes)

- Read and talk about the title and author of the book.
- Check out the cover and blurb.
- Possible questions: *Where do you think the story takes place? How would you describe what's happening? Can you predict what the story is going to be about?*
- Discuss the type of text and clues that let us know it's a mystery.
- Make connections to other mysteries students have read.
- Briefly discuss what they already know about the characteristics of the mystery genre (list ideas on a chart).
- State purpose for reading: *Today, we're going to read pages 1–6. Then we'll stop and talk about what we've read. As you read, see if you can figure out who's the main character/detective and what the crime is that needs to be solved. Also, see if you can figure out how the main character knows there's a crime in the first place. Use your blue sticky-notes to flag the parts that tell you that information. If you come to any words you don't know and can't figure out, jot those down on your yellow sticky-note.*
- Shele charts the following questions for students to refer to during their reading:
  - *Who is the main character/detective?*
  - *What is the crime to be solved?*
  - *How did the detective learn about the crime?*
  - *What other important information did you learn?*

(continued on next page)

During Reading: Students Read the Text (approximately 10–12 minutes)

- Listen to Tulia read aloud. Make teaching points as necessary and check for understanding.
- Discuss any information students have flagged.
- Visually check engagement of other four students and how they are progressing in their reading.

After Reading: Return to the Focus and Dig Deeper (approximately 5–7 minutes)

- Discuss what students have found out based on their reading so far.
- Have students talk about where they placed their sticky-notes and why.
- Return to the focus to confirm the answers to the four questions on the chart.
- Discuss any words students were unable to figure out on their own. Use whiteboard.
- Have students update their predictions for what will happen next.
- Tell students to read to page 12 independently. Set purpose for next portion of reading. *As you read, see if your predictions were right or whether you'll need to change your thinking. Also, use your sticky-note to flag any new clues you pick up as you read. Remember to keep track of any tricky words you can't figure out. Okay, readers, you can go any place in the room or back to your desk to read.*
- Listen to Michael read aloud. Make teaching points as necessary and check for understanding.
- Discuss any flagged information.
- Visually check engagement of other four students and how they are progressing in their reading.

DAY TWO

- Give students 10 minutes prior to meeting as a group to review and refresh their memories by quickly skimming the section they read the day before so they will be ready for a discussion.
- Meet to discuss portion of text read.
- Discuss the purpose for reading, new information gathered from the reading, clues right there in the book, and clues that require the reader to infer. Have students return to the text to support thinking and/or provide proof.
- Have students update their predictions.
- Assign next portion of reading.

Shele Banford meets with five of her third-grade students to support them as they learn how to keep track of characters, events, clues and to make inferences in a short mystery chapter book during guided reading.

TIPS AND TECHNIQUES

Practicing Inferencing Skills with Mysteries

Students love reading mysteries, and they're great for practicing inferencing skills. Here's a list of some popular mystery series:

A to Z Mysteries by Ron Roy (Random House)

American Girl History Mysteries (various authors) (American Girl)

The Boxcar Children Mysteries by Gertrude Chandler Warner (Albert Whitman & Co)

Cam Jansen Mysteries by David A. Adler (Puffin)

Carmen Sandiego Mysteries by Melissa Peterson (HarperCollins)

Encyclopedia Brown Mysteries by Donald J. Sobol (Bantam)

Herculeah Jones Mysteries by Betsy Byars (Puffin)

Nate the Great Mysteries by Marjorie Weinman Sharmat (Random House)

Sammy Keyes Mysteries by Wendelin Van Draanen (Random House)

The Sisters Grimm Mysteries by Michael Buckley (Harry N. Abrams)

Students can also check out this Web site:

MysteryNet's Kids Mysteries at http://kids.mysterynet.com

Series books are wonderful materials for use with at-risk readers. Series books are easier than a variety of books because the reader builds up a store of information about the characters and the author's style that make the books predictable.

—Patricia Cunningham and Richard Allington, *Classrooms That Work: They Can All Read and Write*

Final Thoughts

When planning for and teaching guided reading lessons, let students' needs instruct you. Because time is limited, it's important to be well organized and prepared for the lesson before meeting with the group. Refer to any anecdotal notes from the most recent lessons and/or individual reading conferences to help plan the focus for the next lesson. Choose a text that will build on the readers' current processing strengths and meet their instructional needs. Think about how you will introduce the text before reading; which students, if any, you will observe during reading; and how the purpose for reading will help direct the discussion after reading. It may help to keep some general ideas in mind when planning for and teaching a guided reading lesson. Ask yourself these questions:

1. What are the learners' needs?

2. What is the focus of the lesson, based on these needs?

3. What text will help teach the students what they need to learn, providing substantial support and a few challenges?

4. How can I connect what I've already taught through read-alouds or shared reading to students' current learning?

5. How will I explicitly state the focus for students at the beginning of the lesson?

6. How does the reading/focus link to the local curriculum? to state standards?

7. How will I make talk an integral part of the lesson before, possibly during, and after reading?

8. Which students will I observe closely during the lesson? Which students will I listen to as they read aloud?

9. How will I extend thinking and understanding once we've returned to the focus of the lesson after the text reading?

In the next chapter, I take a look at the comprehension strategies proficient readers employ when they encounter text. Knowing how these strategies work will allow you to more fully contribute to appropriate and effective instruction. Helping your students learn and use these strategies will enable them to become competent, skilled readers.

Chapter 4

Mary meets with four third-grade students to compare the similarities and differences of two nonfiction books they've read during their guided reading lessons.

Exploring Key Reading Strategies in Guided Reading

An important aspect of reading comprehension instruction is being able to make our own comprehension practices visible in order to help students understand how we, as competent readers, understand what we are reading. As fluent, capable readers, our reading comprehension practices are largely invisible to us. One of the primary challenges for us as teachers of reading is to learn to model our comprehension practices for our students.

—Frank Serafini, *Lessons in Comprehension*

Proficient readers use multiple reading strategies—invisible, "in-the-head" processes—to make meaning from print as they navigate texts. What's more, proficient readers know that they need to use these strategies *before*, *during*, and *after* reading as they think their way through the texts they read. Because guided reading groups allow you to work with students in a small, focused setting and to help your readers during the lesson, they provide an ideal opportunity for exploring reading strategies. They offer you the chance to observe a reader's behaviors, gather evidence to determine which strategies he or she is using, and then attend to those specific strategies. The key reading comprehension strategies are so fundamental to successful reading that I've dedicated this full chapter to their coverage.

Examining Your Own Reading Strategies

Before looking further at teaching reading strategies to your students within your guided reading groups, I think it will be helpful to consider what happens when a proficient reader picks up a book, a newspaper, or a magazine to read. If you focus on your own reading behaviors, not only will you become more mindful of what is by now automatic for you but you will also develop a better feeling for the strategies that you can model for your students during guided reading lessons.

As a proficient reader, you know how a particular text type works and how to think and use that text, based on your prior experiences and knowledge of the world. You know how to determine what is most important as you read and what to do when meaning breaks down. As readers, we use these *learned* systems of strategies so automatically that we give them little thought or attention. Our systems are so well established that we are able to put the majority of our focus on the meaning of the text, only rarely needing to attend to word solving. Not until we slow down and take notice of what it is we are doing as readers can we begin to better help the readers we teach.

To think about how we use strategies as we read, take a moment to read the following text. Pay special attention to what you're doing mentally as you read and maneuver through the text. You may want to get a colleague to read the passage so you can examine your thought processes together and talk about what you did as a reader to understand the text.

Joe Cool

Today is going to be beautiful. I awaken to warbling and the cheery glow of sunlight streaming through nylon walls. I lie in my bag, imagining the sweetness that awaits: the miles of empty trail, the triumph of switchbacks tamed, the bracing dip in an alpine lake, the hearty Asian dinner and starry dessert. It's going to be an epic.

Truth be told I depend on morning joe, whether I'm sitting on a log in the Sierra or slumped on my couch or watching *SportsCenter*. Yet there's no denying that this cherished ritual assumes exalted status in the wild. One whiff of the aromatic grounds awakens your senses; instantly, the scent of pine needles and sweet mountain air comes to the fore. You taste the ebony nectar, lingering on its smoky goodness, and everything—the piercing morning light, 3-day-old bread, even your grumpy buddies—takes on a softer edge. It's as if you've traded in your old Trinitron for a spanking new HDTV.

("Joe Cool: An Ode to Backcountry Coffee" by Peter Flax is reprinted from *Backpacker* magazine, December 2003 issue.)

Reflect on the ways in which you had to actively bring understandings to the text in order to make sense of it. What happened as you read? What did you notice about yourself as a reader? How did your thinking and understanding change as you read and gathered more information?

As you read the title, you may have thought the passage was going to be about a cool guy named Joe, rather than an ode to morning coffee. If so, what did you read along the way that made you change your original prediction? Did you reread or skip ahead when you were aware the meaning wasn't clear? When you read, "the cheery glow of sunlight was streaming through nylon walls. I lie in my bag . . . ," you may have asked yourself, Where is this person? You probably quickly figured out that the author was camping and the sounds of the birds warbling were just outside his tent as he lay in his sleeping bag.

As the author ticked off his plans for the day, did you visualize any of them—hiking mountain switchback trails or plunging into an alpine lake? Did you flash back to a time in your own life when the smell of coffee greeted you in the morning as you woke up in pine-filled woods? Did you wonder how or where a "hearty Asian dinner" would take place? And what did you make of the analogy between HDTV and the effects of a cup of joe?

Maybe you agree with the author's perspective when it comes to this cherished ritual. Or maybe, like me, you're not a coffee drinker, and if so, you found yourself connecting to something equally satisfying instead.

What you no doubt did as you read the passage was to dip into your working repertoire of strategies and bring them together to make meaning of the text. It is this *system of strategies* readers use to gain and maintain meaning when reading.

Reflecting on your own strategic actions as a reader gives you insight into the variety of strategies you use to make meaning. We cannot see these strategies, but we know they are being used because the reader is processing and comprehending text. Keeping in mind the strategies that students need to learn and employ as readers gives your instruction focus.

The Process of Reading: A System of Strategies

Proficient readers quickly and efficiently use a complex network of strategies they've developed to actively process information to make meaning of what they read. (See chart starting on page 72.) Competent readers are aware when meaning breaks down, and they do something to fix the breakdown and restore meaning. Keep in mind that proficient readers do not use one strategy at a time. Rather, as they read, *many strategies operate simultaneously*. In fact, you probably used a number of the strategies or actions listed below when you read "Joe Cool." Proficient readers use strategies quite unconsciously as they move through the reading and processing of a text. These strategic actions might include the following:

- Predicting
- Searching
- Checking
- Confirming
- Self-correcting
- Monitoring
- Solving words
- Adjusting
- Maintaining fluency

These strategic actions help keep the reading going forward; they help the reader *sustain* the reading of the text (Fountas and Pinnell, 2001a). If meaning breaks down during reading, proficient readers have a variety of fix-up strategies they know to try to solve errors. We can observe the reader's behavior as evidence of strategic actions.

Readers also use a system of strategies for understanding or thinking about what they read. Fountas and Pinnell (2001a) refer to these strategies as those that *expand* meaning for the readers. They write, "[S]trategies for expanding meaning allow readers to go beyond the specific text that is being processed" (p. 319). Such excellent books as *Mosaic of Thought* (Keene and Zimmermann, 1997) and *Strategies That Work* (Harvey and Goudvis, 2000) explore the importance of explicitly teaching students these comprehension strategies to help them construct meaning in their minds as they read.

Readers construct meaning and expand understanding using the following additional strategic actions:

- Making connections
- Questioning

- Visualizing

- Inferring

- Determining importance

- Summarizing

- Synthesizing

- Analyzing

- Evaluating and critiquing

Look at the Key Strategies in the Process of Reading graphic on the next page, adapted from the strategy work of Fountas and Pinnell (2001a), to get a better sense of how a reader actively and continuously draws on multiple strategies to process and comprehend a text. The "reader" is situated in the middle to illustrate how, she integrates available strategies to work out the meaning of the text. The reader applies these strategies before, during, and after reading to help her comprehend the text beyond a literal level. The efficient and effective use of these strategies makes the reading fluent and enhances the level of comprehension.

Comprehension is what a child is doing when holding a conversation with someone, listening to someone reading aloud, or reading on his or her own, at any time or place. Comprehension lies in what learners say, what is read to them, and what they read and write; learners should know that all literacy acts involve comprehension.

—Marie M. Clay, *By Different Paths to Common Outcomes*

Key Strategies in the Process of Reading

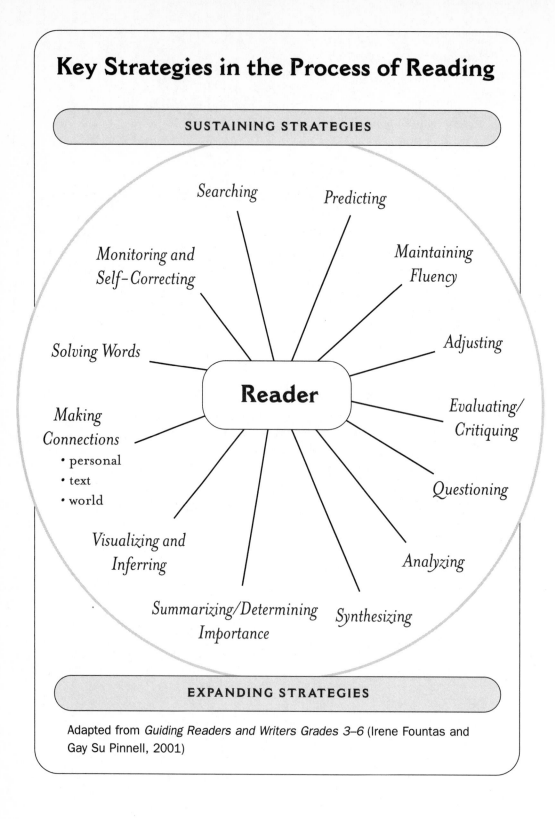

SUSTAINING STRATEGIES

Searching

Predicting

Monitoring and
Self-Correcting

Maintaining
Fluency

Solving Words

Adjusting

Reader

Evaluating/
Critiquing

Making
Connections
• personal
• text
• world

Questioning

Visualizing and
Inferring

Analyzing

Summarizing/Determining
Importance

Synthesizing

EXPANDING STRATEGIES

Adapted from *Guiding Readers and Writers Grades 3–6* (Irene Fountas and
Gay Su Pinnell, 2001)

Differentiating Skills and Strategies

What's the difference between a strategy and a skill? Strategies are best understood as the mental processes or "in the head" operations we use as we read. As discussed earlier, readers use various strategies, or cognitive actions, to derive meaning from the texts they read. Some of the strategic actions readers learn to use simultaneously and quite flexibly to solve words and understand texts include searching, predicting, checking, confirming, monitoring, making connections, questioning, visualizing, inferring, and determining importance. These strategies are part of a working system proficient readers develop over time and readily draw upon as they read. Readers who struggle may not have developed an effective strategic system to construct meaning or may be reading texts that are too hard, causing their working repertoire of strategies to break down due to the high demands of the texts.

Skills are different from strategies. Skills are related to item knowledge—such as recognizing affixes and root words, syllabication, or knowing how to use the table of contents—that readers use to support their ability to read. Both strategies and skills are important for readers to learn; however, in this chapter the focus is on the teaching of strategies because they are what readers use to construct meaning as they process and comprehend text.

Let's take a closer look at "skills" versus "strategy" teaching to better understand the difference. Teaching a skill often focuses on the *what* or *how*. For example, I can teach students *what* a table of contents is and *how* to use it. That's a teachable skill and an item they can learn. But not only do I want students to know *what* a table of contents is and *how* to use it, I want them to understand *when* and *why* a reader would use the table of contents to extract important information and essential ideas in nonfiction before, during, or after reading. Strategy teaching focuses more on the *when* and *why* of reading and addresses the inner processing and thinking readers engage in to make sense of what they read. Students need to be both strategic and skilled to become competent readers. Guided reading is a place where we can teach both.

Summary of Reading Strategies:
From Teacher Talk to Reader's Inner Talk

The chart on pages 72–78 explains why each of the sustaining and expanding strategies is important, and suggests the instruction that may occur when highlighting and teaching for a particular strategy as well as the nature of the inner conversations we want to foster in strategic readers. We help readers develop and use these in-the-head strategies by demonstrating effective ways of working with texts and by prompting and reminding them to employ them. Although it's critical that time is spent reading, teaching, and conferring with students, our ultimate goal is to encourage readers to internalize the kinds of questions and talk that we use when working with them so they can refine and expand their ever-increasing inner control over the reading process.

Strategic Action	Definition	Why It Is Important	Teacher Talk	Reader's Inner Talk: How It May Sound
Searching	Seeking out and taking in the important information from the text and putting it together.	Readers need to attend to the print and take notice of the sources of information available to them, including the print features, as they process the text and construct meaning. They search the text to gather information at the letter, word, sentence, or text level.	• You said _____. • Does it make sense? • Does it sound right? • Does it look right? • What did you notice when you reread? • As you skimmed and scanned, what helped you decide what text type this is? • How did the author make the important points stand out for the reader? • What are the different ways the reader could go about reading this particular text?	• I said _____. • Does it make sense to me? • Does it sound right to me? • Does it look right to me? • When I reread I noticed . . . • As I skimmed and scanned, the parts that helped me decide the text type were . . . • I'm thinking the author made the important points stand out for me by . . .
Predicting	Anticipating words, phrases, and text structures based on knowledge of language and the meaning of the text read so far. Using prior knowledge to anticipate what	Readers need to continually anticipate, confirm, and revise their predictions as they read.	• What do you think this text will be about? • What do you think you will learn? • What do you think will happen next? • What have you already read that makes you think that? • Using what you've read,	• I think this text will be about . . . • I think I might learn . . . • Based on what has happened so far, I'm thinking the next thing that will happen will be . . . • What I have already read that makes me think that is . . .

(continued on next page)

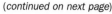

Strategic Action	Definition	Why It Is Important	Teacher Talk	Reader's Inner Talk: How It May Sound
	will happen in the text before, during, and after reading.		what do you think that word might mean?	• Based on what I've read, I think that word might mean . . .

Monitoring and Self-Correcting	Checking understanding of what is read at all times to make sure reading makes sense, sounds right, and looks right. Self-correcting as needed for meaning and accuracy.	Readers need to use all sources of information when reading—meaning, language structure, and visual information in print. They need to know when meaning breaks down and which missing, neglected, or additional information to use to correct the response.	• What did you notice?
			• Check to see if what you read . . .
			  • makes sense.
			  • sounds right.
			  • looks right.
			• What did you do when you got confused?
			• How did you help yourself when you didn't understand that part?
			• What new information did you learn?
				• I noticed . . .
				• I need to check to see if what I read . . .
				  • makes sense.
				  • sounds right.
				  • looks right.
				• When I got confused I . . .
				• When I didn't understand that part, I decided to . . .
				• From reading this piece I learned . . .

Maintaining Fluency	Reading and processing text at a good rate; using phrasing and expression as it relates to the meaning in the text; pausing appropriately; using suitable voice or inflection for punctuation.	Fluency supports the readers' anticipation of meaning, which directly relates to comprehension.	• Try rereading that part and make it sound like someone is talking. • How would the character say that? • How do you think the author would want the reader to read that part? • What in the text helped you know how to read that part? • How would the intended meaning change if we stressed the word ___?	• I'll try rereading that part and make it sound like someone is talking. • The character would say that like this . . . • The author would want me to read that part like this . . . • I knew how to read that part of the text because I noticed . . . • I know it would show she's scared if I said it like this . . .
Adjusting	Speeding up or slowing the rate of reading depending on the purpose and the difficulty of the text.	Readers need to approach reading tasks in different ways and make adjustments as they read depending on the purpose for	• Which parts required you to slow down and read more carefully? • Where did you reread in order to understand better? How did that help you?	• I slowed down and read more carefully when . . . • The part I needed to reread in order to understand better was . . .

(continued on next page)

Strategic Action	Definition	Why It Is Important	Teacher Talk	Reader's Inner Talk: How It May Sound
		reading and the text difficulty.	• How did you skim the text to find the information you needed? Then, how did you read that part of the text? • How did stopping to turn and talk to a partner during reading help you think about what you read? • What parts did you read slowly or reread to appreciate the author's use of language?	• How should I go about reading this particular text? • How can I skim the text to find the information I need?
Solving Words	Integrating visual, phonological, meaning, and structural information effectively and efficiently to figure out new words and miscued familiar words in order to maintain meaning in a text.	Readers need to analyze words rapidly using letters, letter clusters, syllable breaks, word parts, and root words while they read so their attention can be directed to the meaning of the text. As readers use "known items" of word knowledge to help construct new knowledge, they extend their processing systems.	• Does that make sense? [after word solving] • Have you seen that word before? • Do you know part of that word? • Does that word look like another word you know? • What do you think that word means from what you've already read?	• Does that make sense? • Have I seen that word before? • I know part of that word. • That word looks like another word I know. • What do I think that word means from what I've already read?
Making Connections	Linking text to one's own experience or life, to other texts, or to one's knowledge of the larger world. Utilizing what is known about how particular	Readers are more likely to understand what they read when they think about information in a text in relation to what they have experienced, read, and know. Readers are more likely to understand what they read when	• What do you already know about that topic that you can think about as you read this text? • How did that connection help you understand more about what you read? • How has your thinking changed based on what you know and have read?	• What do I already know about the topic that I can think about as I read this text? • How did that connection help me understand more about what I read? • My thinking changed because I know _____ and I read _____.

(continued on next page)

Strategic Action	Definition	Why It Is Important	Teacher Talk	Reader's Inner Talk: How It May Sound
	features work in different texts.	they recognize the kind of text it is and literary features it contains.	• What other texts have you read that help you to understand more about this text? • What is the author's purpose for setting up the text this way for the reader?	• What other texts have I read that help me understand more about this text? • I think the author's purpose for setting up the text this way for the reader might be . . .
Questioning	Generating questions before, during, and after reading.	Readers generate questions to frame their thinking as they read, build meaning, locate specific information, clarify sources of confusion, and expand new understandings.	• What does the title of this text make you wonder about even before reading it? • What questions do you have so far? • Where did you find the answers? • How did your questions help you understand this text? • What questions weren't answered and how can you go about finding the answers?	• After reading the title I'm wondering . . . • What questions do I have so far? • I know where to look to find the answers to my questions. • My questions helped me understand more about _____ by . . . • What questions weren't answered and how can I go about finding the answers?
Visualizing	Creating mental images before, during, and after reading.	Readers create images to help them recall, remember, interpret, clarify, and enhance what is read.	• How do you think the author's details help the reader to understand more about _____? • How did the images in your head help you clarify and understand what you read? • How did your images change as you read and learned more? • How did you adjust your images after reading and listening to the responses and shared images of other readers? • Is there another way that you could picture this happening?	• The author's details helped me understand more about _____ by . . . • The pictures in my head helped me understand . . . • In the beginning I pictured it this way . . . Later, I changed how I pictured it when I read . . . • After talking about what I read with the group, I pictured the character differently. • Is there another way that I could picture this happening?

(continued on next page)

Strategic Action	Definition	Why It Is Important	Teacher Talk	Reader's Inner Talk: How It May Sound
Inferring	Using background knowledge and the information in the text to draw conclusions or make assumptions beyond what is explicitly stated in the text.	Readers need to integrate what they already know with information from the text to "read between the lines," or make reasoned assumptions not explicitly stated in the text, illustrations, photographs, or graphic organizers.	• What information can you gather from studying the illustration? • What was the missing information the author wanted the reader to fill in? What makes you think so? • Explain your thinking and how you came to that conclusion. • What was the author's purpose for writing this selection/book?	• Just by looking at the illustration I know . . . • What was the missing information the author wanted me to fill in? What makes me think so? • This information makes me think . . . • Perhaps the author's purpose for writing this selection/book was . . .
Determining Importance	Deciding what is key or important information at the word, sentence, or text level when reading.	Readers need to be able to distinguish important from unimportant information when reading. They need to identify key ideas, details, themes, text structures, and text features to help them decide what is and is not essential in the text.	• What important information did you gather from (this part of) the text? • What key words or phrases signaled importance to you? How did you indicate this for yourself? • What information did you already know and what was new to you? • How did deciding what your purpose was for reading this text help you focus on the important information? • How did the author organize this text to help the reader focus on important ideas/information?	• What important information did I gather from (this part of) the text? • The key words or phrases that signaled importance to me were . . . The way I indicated this for myself was . . . • What information did I already know and what was new to me? • Reading the captions helped me focus on some of the important information. • How did the author organize this text to help me focus on important ideas/information?
Summarizing	Condensing information, either during or after reading, into the general	Readers need to be able to select and organize essential events, concepts, ideas,	• How did you help yourself put together the important pieces of information/ events as you read?	• How did I help myself put together the important pieces of information/events as I read?

(continued on next page)

Strategic Action	Definition	Why It Is Important	Teacher Talk	Reader's Inner Talk: How It May Sound
	ideas or main points.	and information during and after reading. As readers process the text, they need to be aware of which parts of the text they need to attend to most. Summarizing helps readers to rethink their reading and understandings.	• What are three key ideas you learned about this topic? • How would you organize the main points so you could remember them? • How did the text type and signal words the author used throughout the text help you to summarize? • How do you think the author would summarize this paragraph/section/chapter/book?	• Three key ideas I learned about this topic are . . . • I organized the main points so I could remember them by . . . • I can borrow the author's words *first*, *next*, *then*, and *finally* to help myself summarize the sequence of what happened. • Perhaps the author would summarize this paragraph/section/chapter/book by saying . . .
Synthesizing	Integrating the words and ideas in a text with existing personal thoughts, knowledge, and questions to gain new understanding.	Readers need to put together important information in a text with their existing background knowledge, opinions, beliefs, and understandings to form new ideas, thinking, perspectives, and insights.	• How did what you read in the text match up/not match up with what you already know? • What new viewpoints are you coming away with? • How has your opinion about this topic/character changed? • What do you think the author's overall message is to the reader? Do you agree? Disagree? • Who else would want to read this article/book? Why?	• How did what I read in the text match up/not match up with what I already know? • Some new perspectives I am coming away with include . . . • My opinion about this topic/character changed based on . . . • I think the author's overall message to the reader is . . . because . . . I agree/disagree because . . . • Who else would want to read this article/book? Why?
Analyzing	Examining elements of texts to better understand their organization, features, and characteristics before, during,	Readers need to become familiar with how texts are constructed and in what ways the features of different text types can help support their understanding and	• What are some of the features you expect to encounter in this type of text? • How is this text like/unlike one you've already read? • How did the graphic	• Some of the features I expect to encounter in this type of text include . . . • How is this text like/unlike another text I've already read? • How did the graphic

(continued on next page)

Strategic Action	Definition	Why It Is Important	Teacher Talk	Reader's Inner Talk: How It May Sound
	and after reading. Investigating the essential features or parts that make up the text as a whole.	communicate meaning in an integrated way.	features help increase your understanding beyond the text? • What do you know now that you didn't know before? • How did the way the author organized the text help you understand it? • What is the purpose of this text as a whole? Is there more than one purpose?	features increase my understanding beyond the text? • After reading that part I learned . . . • How did the way the author organized the text help me understand? • I'm thinking the purpose of this text as a whole is . . . There may be more than one purpose.
Evaluating/ Critiquing	Reflecting and making judgments about the text during and after reading.	Readers need to take a reflective stance to evaluate and critique the author's purpose and how the information is presented in the texts they read. They need to consider their own response to the text.	• How can you use the information you read? • How did the information in this text sort out your thinking and inform your opinions? • What else could the author have included in the text that would have helped the reader's understanding? • Whose point of view was heard in this text? Are there viewpoints not heard? • Do you think the author provides a fair representation of the issue, topic, or character? Why? Why not?	• How can I use the information I read? • How did the information in this text clarify my thinking and change or support my opinions? • What else could the author have included in the text that would have helped my understanding? • Whose viewpoint was heard in this text? Are there viewpoints that weren't heard? • Do I think the author provides a fair representation of the issue, topic, or character? Why? Why not?

Using Just-Right Texts

If you want students to employ sustaining strategies in the midst of reading, it's critical that you (and your students) select texts that provide only a few challenges. Remember, in order for readers to maintain the forward momentum of reading and attend to the meaning of the text, they need to be able to read long stretches of text so that quick, coordinated problem solving can occur at points of difficulty.

Take time to observe your students as they read aloud short passages from just-right texts. Watch for them to be able to read long stretches of text, stopping only briefly to use "fix-up" strategies that monitor and correct their reading. The reader's working system of strategies helps him to maintain that forward momentum as he moves through the reading of the text, only stopping briefly to problem-solve and then continue on (Clay, 2001).

You will see the adverse effect when students attempt to orally read texts that are too challenging. The reader's strategic processes often begin to break down when a large portion of the reading work is given over to solving words. This breakdown impacts the reader's ability to maintain fluency. It becomes an act of "getting through" the reading of the text, which frequently shifts the reader's focus and energy away from the meaning of the text to just reading the words.

Some suggested guided reading book titles:

Amazing Animals by Kate Boehm Jerome

Amusement Park Science by Dan Greenberg

Bats Have Hands by Wendy Blaxland

Exploring Space by Robert Coupe

A Brand of Brave Men: The Story of the 54th Massachusetts Regiment by Ellen Dreyer

Discovering the Titanic by Cindy Trumbore

Galileo Man of Science by Keri O'Donnell

The World of Water by Susan Paris

Twisters, Tornadoes and Other Wild Weather by Pamela Graham

Great Inventions and Where They Came From by Jackie Glassman

Final Thoughts

Most intermediate students have developed a good sense of the reading process but are still refining their strategies as they encounter more difficult and varied texts. In our guided reading work in the intermediate grades, it is our job as teachers to literally guide these older readers toward applying the key reading strategies to increasingly sophisticated texts over time. Keep in mind that upper-grade readers use many of the same strategies that beginning readers use, or, for that matter, that you and I use. What differs are the levels of expertise and sophistication in the use of these strategies as more complex texts are encountered (Fountas and Pinnell, 2001a).

Proficient readers have thoughts and ideas in their heads as they read. They don't just let the words wash over them and let it go at that. Rather, they bring their strategies, understandings, and ideas to the text and approximate the author's intent in order to get meaning from it. They transact with the text in order to understand it (Rosenblatt, 1978). The graphic below illustrates this process.

How We Make Meaning

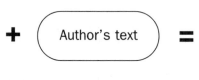

As teachers, we need to create the context for our students to think about and extract meaning from what they read and encounter in text. Our teaching, conversations, and reading work with students need to reinforce this idea while we explicitly teach and guide them to employ these interconnected strategies to understand what they read.

In the next chapter, I describe how elements like classroom arrangement, predictable workshop routines and procedures, and resources such as the classroom library and school book room all contribute to purposeful, worthwhile reading instruction and learning. I describe the three basic components of a reading workshop—the mini-lesson, reading time, and share time. I also describe what the other students are doing when you are meeting with a group of students in guided reading groups or in individual reading conferences.

Chapter 5

Shele Banford's classroom environment supports whole- and small-group instruction as well as individual student conferences. Here Shele meets with a guided reading group while other students read independently.

Organizing and Managing the Classroom Environment for Literacy Instruction

Children need a supportive environment in which to develop as readers. Whether this means creating a safe place to make mistakes or allowing children the extra time they need to develop, they need space. . . . The design of our workshop should not restrict opportunities; rather, it should create space for children to interact with caring, supportive teachers and peers in a learning community.

—Frank Serafini, *The Reading Workshop*

Not long ago I read an article that described how in some schools in Italy there are two teachers in every classroom. Interestingly, the article went on to explain that these teachers actually contended that each classroom had *three* teachers. The "third teacher" was the arrangement or design of the classroom environment. The classroom arrangement has the capacity to function as a discrete yet vital support system for the teaching of reading. It can either hinder or enhance teaching. In order to spend long stretches of time reading in ways that incorporate the instruction during the mini-lesson, guided reading, and individual reading conferences, students need to work in a highly structured yet responsive environment.

Consider the fact that you and your students spend six to seven hours in the classroom each day. Think about the space and how the arrangement of it can provide comfort yet be a place where students can do their best work and you can do your optimum teaching.

Each classroom setting is different. Take a thorough look at your classroom environment as you decide on the optimum arrangement for your own situation. You may find it helpful to ask yourself these essential questions:

- Can I picture myself working with students in the classroom areas—in whole-group lessons, small groups, and individually?

- Where and when will I meet for guided reading and individual conferences?

- Are the students able to move comfortably between work areas?

- Does the room have an area where students can work quietly and another area away from it where productive discussions can occur?

- How will I create and maintain opportunities for students to participate in informal conversations, book talks, and discussions about their work, their learning, and their lives?

- How much of the classroom is student-generated?

- Is there evidence on the walls that important thinking and work about reading and writing is going on in the classroom?

- Are books, supplies, and materials organized and easily accessible for instruction near the locations in which they will be used?

- What are my expectations for students' work, behavior, and interactions? How will I make these expectations clear to students?

- What consequences will I put in place when students fail to meet expectations?

Set Up a Predictable Framework for Reading Workshop

If you think about it, the rhythms of daily life in a classroom are much like those outside the classroom. Routines and rituals are fundamental to our days, but we also look for a degree of novelty and surprise. In the classroom, too, there must be a certain amount of flexibility yet a high degree of predictability and continuity for students from day to day. Establish the look and tone of the classroom at the beginning of the school year to support the work that the students and you will be doing during reading workshop. You will also be supporting their growing independence as readers. Mini-lessons at the beginning of the year center on

Students gather for a mini-lesson in a large meeting area for short stretches of 10–15 minutes of reading instruction at the beginning of the workshop. This area also serves as a place to gather at the end of the workshop to share how students made use of the idea from the day's mini-lesson and to evaluate the learning that has taken place. Teaching materials near the meeting area include a large easel or whiteboard, chart paper, markers, different size sticky-notes, and an overhead projector.

A table or area on the floor for small-group instruction by the classroom teacher and/or resource teacher provides a supportive area for reading instruction during the workshop time. Books and materials are close by.

Desks or tables are clustered in groups so students can easily confer and collaborate with one another.

A comfortable classroom library with a carpet, pillows, a small couch or winged chair, and shelves of books in baskets for easy accessibility for perusing or book selection takes up a corner of the room. Students gather there to read independently or with a buddy during reading workshop.

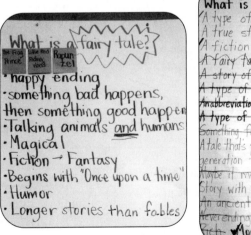

Computers for reading bookmarked Web sites and a listening station with books on tape support literacy learning.

Literacy charts generated by the teacher and students together capture the thinking and learning readers do during reading workshop.

Involving Students in Setting Up the Classroom Workplace

Although the room arrangement needs to be well thought-out and functional, it need not be elaborate. Consider the fact that you don't have to do it all by yourself. More and more teachers with whom I work are engaging students to assist in the design of the classroom community where they will be learning and working together for the whole year. Students are greeted with signs on the door saying "Construction to begin soon. Waiting for sharp thinkers and hard workers." Or, "The Great Work Begins on September 2! Counting on YOUR creative ideas, talent, and flair." This shared effort to create the workplace supports students' learning. In addition, sharing the responsibility for classroom design saves you time and gives students real ownership of the place where they will learn and grow for an entire school year.

developing routines that help students use the reading workshop in purposeful and productive ways. Students need to be clear about how to use the time when you are not working with them. Keep in mind that when you devote time to teaching about how things work in the classroom, you will be able to spend more time teaching and less and less time managing problems as the year progresses.

The Basic Components of Reading Workshop

Establishing routines and setting up a predictable reading workshop structure with specific components at the outset supports teaching and learning all year long. Students get the most out of a learning community when they have a clear sense of how it functions. The learners in your classroom need to understand their roles and responsibilities in reading workshop so they can focus and accomplish what they need to during that time. Additionally, having expected routines and workshop components in place helps set the stage for small-group guided reading.

> In ancient crafts workshop, the teacher was a master craftsperson who demonstrated a trade and coached apprentices in the context of making real products for the community. In contemporary classrooms, we borrow the workshop metaphor to create reading workshops where students get a large chunk of time to practice the trade of reading . . . while teachers take on the new roles of mentors, coaches, and models.
>
> —Harvey Daniels and Marilyn Bizar, *Teaching the Best Practice Way: Methods That Matter, K–12*

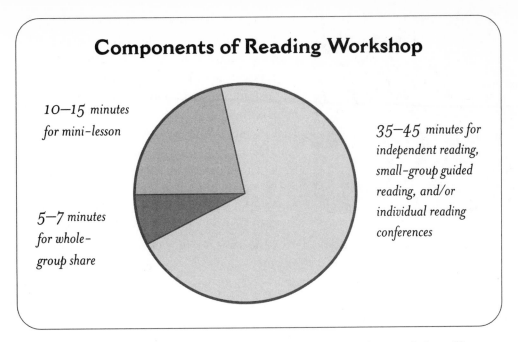

Components of Reading Workshop

10–15 minutes for mini-lesson

35–45 minutes for independent reading, small-group guided reading, and/or individual reading conferences

5–7 minutes for whole-group share

Plan to schedule a minimum of one hour each day for reading workshop. Three basic components should be present in a reading workshop: (1) time for whole-group mini-lessons, which often include shared reading or an interactive read-aloud; (2) time for independent reading, small-group guided reading, and/or individual reading conferences; and (3) time for whole-group sharing.

The Mini-Lesson

Typically the reading workshop begins with students gathered in the meeting area of the classroom for a short mini-lesson of about 10–15 minutes. All mini-lessons should be planned and have a specific focus based on your ongoing assessments of students during guided reading *and* individual reading conferences. At the beginning of the school year, as assessment begins to take place, mini-lessons often center around procedures and routines for the hour-long workshop, such as sharing one's reading identity, using and caring for books in the classroom library, self-

---

TIPS AND TECHNIQUES

Establish a Schedule Students Can Count On

It's important that students know when the reading workshop is scheduled so they are ready to engage in reading work. When students can count on a certain amount of time to read each day, they can more easily pick up where they left off the previous day and can better plan a good stopping point in their reading for the next day.

Rachel King reads a content-related Big Book with her third-grade students during a shared reading mini-lesson at the beginning of reading workshop.

selecting just-right books, and advertising interesting and worthy selections through book talks—given by both you and the students. Once the routines are well established the mini-lessons often shift to strategy and skill instruction. (For more on reading strategies, see Chapter 4.)

The mini-lesson is often taught with either a read-aloud or a shared reading text. A picture book, trade book, or short excerpt from a novel is selected for a read-aloud lesson. A Big Book used at the easel or a lifted text placed on the overhead projector makes a good choice for shared reading. Often, but not always, the same strategy or skill in the mini-lesson becomes the central point of instruction in guided reading instruction and/or individual reading conferences.

Possible Mini-Lessons

Mini-lessons are short, specific, and direct. They most often arise from students' needs. The following list is not a checklist, nor is it comprehensive; rather, it is a list of possible mini-lessons you may teach. Because many of the suggestions are broad and multi-layered, some skills and strategies will need to be taught over a long period of time, while others will require only a quick lesson or two. Be careful to avoid teaching too much in one mini-lesson. Consider what will best move your readers forward.

> Guidelines for Reading Workshop
> 1. Everyone reads.
> 2. Keep it quiet if you're reading.
> 3. Use a whisper voice if you're conferring with a teacher.
> 4. Read *just right* books that use your thinking and reading muscles *just a little bit.*
> 5. Know your reading goal.

E.J. Green generated a list of reading workshop guidelines at the beginning of the year with his fifth-grade students.

> **EASY**
> • I know all the words.
> • I'm focused + I understand what I am reading.
> • I feel relaxed + comfortable.
> • My reading muscle is working a little bit.
> • I'm not learning much new at all.

> **JUST RIGHT**
> • I know almost all words.
> • I am interested + focused.
> • I understand, but may have to stop occasionally.
> • I still feel relaxed + comfortable.
> • My reading muscle is working a little harder.
> • I learn the most.

> **CHALLENGING**
> • May not know many words.
> • I am stressed and confused.
> • I stop a lot to clarify.
> • I may not have much prior knowledge.
> • My reading muscle is working way too hard.
> • I may not remember what I just read.

Dana Moury's fourth-grade class generated a list of criteria for easy, just-right, and challenging books together at the beginning of the school year.

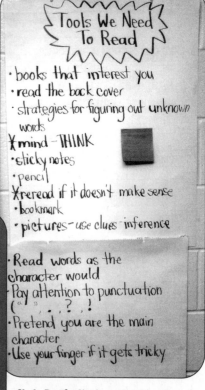

> Tools We Need To Read
> • books that interest you
> • read the back cover
> • strategies for figuring out unknown words
> • mind - THINK
> • sticky notes
> • pencil
> • reread if it doesn't make sense
> • bookmark
> • pictures - use clues · inference
>
> • Read words as the character would
> • Pay attention to punctuation (" " , . ? . !)
> • Pretend you are the main character
> • Use your finger if it gets tricky

Shele Banford's class created a Tools for Readers chart they added to over time as students noticed ways to help themselves when reading.

Possible Mini-Lessons

Procedures and Routines

- Working according to the basic guidelines of reading workshop
- Organizing, storing, and using classroom library materials
- Caring for books
- Self-selecting appropriate (just-right) books
- Finding a place to read in the classroom during reading workshop
- Signing out books from the class library
- Sustaining reading during workshop time
- Knowing what to do when a book is finished in the middle of the workshop time
- Deciding when to stick with or abandon a book
- Learning the system for keeping, filling out, and storing reading records
- Responding to reading (talking, writing, visual representations, etc.)
- Conferring with the teacher (structure/goals of conference)
- Setting attainable goals
- Reading a variety of genres
- Using "turn and talk" time productively
- Reading with a partner
- Using sticky-notes to mark points of interest, tricky vocabulary, confusion, ideas to discuss
- Making or writing book recommendations
- Giving a book talk
- Using peers and literacy charts as resources if the teacher is working with other students
- Making a schedule of best times to fit reading in at home

Strategies and Skills

- Assuming a reader's identity: "I am a reader!"
- Previewing a book before reading
- Monitoring your own reading and understanding
- Identifying and using fix-up strategies when meaning is lost
- Using comprehension strategies (making connections, questioning, visualizing, inferring, determining importance, summarizing, synthesizing, analyzing, evaluating, and critiquing)
- Searching and locating specific information
- Skimming and scanning text to support ideas
- Identifying key vocabulary
- Using context clues to figure out vocabulary
- Attending to punctuation
- Adjusting reading pace and style based on text difficulty and purpose for reading
- Reading with intonation and expression
- Identifying and discussing author's purpose and/or style
- Comparing and contrasting different perspectives
- Identifying and using literary elements and devices
- Identifying and using nonfiction organizational text structures such as cause and effect, question and answer, and problem and solution
- Identifying and using nonfiction text features such as table of contents, index, and glossary
- Identifying and using poetic forms, features, and language
- Using references and resources
- Identifying strengths and needs as a reader

Create Literacy Charts
with Students

Capture thinking and learning about reading processes and important routines by generating literacy charts with students. When students participate in making classroom charts, they have ownership of them and feel more connected to the information. Charts that describe what to do during reading workshop, how to select a just-right book, ways in which readers solve words, and what readers can do to make sure they understand the author's message serve as reminders and resources of your teaching and learning together. You may try color-coding charts, using one color for each curriculum subject. For example, all reading literacy charts are written in green. Make sure charts for a common curriculum subject have their own area in the room so it is easy to refer to them. Many charts function as "living documents" because they grow and change over time as students gain new understandings and learn more about reading.

If classroom wall space is an issue, consider organizing the literacy charts that are no longer of prime importance into a Big Book reference. You can use rings to bind the edge of the charts to make what looks like a large reference book. Another idea is to cut the charts apart and reorganize them so you can easily glue them into a ready-made, blank Big Book. Include title, table of contents, and page numbers so it's easy to find a particular chart. Refer to them as needed, just as you would any reference source.

Reading Time

After the mini-lesson, the largest section of the reading workshop (about 35–45 minutes) is devoted to students' independent and/or guided reading time. In a workshop environment, unless they are working with you, students spend most of their time reading privately. Students often spread around the room to read from their self-selected just-right books and/or from their guided reading selection. In his book *What Really Matters for Struggling Readers* (2001), Richard Allington reminds us that studies consistently show that making large blocks of time available for students to *simply read* not only builds the volume of reading but also improves reading achievement. Given this rich research evidence, it makes good sense to ensure that this block of the reading workshop is designed for students to spend time reading. While students are reading privately, you are free to conduct small-group guided reading lessons or individual reading conferences.

At the start of the school year, launching the reading workshop takes about four to five weeks. During this time, all the essential components of a comprehensive literacy framework are included in the reading workshop time *except* for guided reading. Because you form guided reading groups based on your assessments, you will not use guided reading in the first weeks of teaching. But you can use read-alouds, shared reading, and independent reading on a daily basis from the start.

In place of meeting with guided reading groups, I initially spend the 35- to 45-minute block moving around the room, looking over students' shoulders at their self-selected books, crouching beside them or pulling up a chair to talk about their reading, or listening and coaching as they read a short portion of the text aloud. I carry a pen, sticky-notes, and a clipboard with a record sheet to jot observations, miscue and anecdotal notations, and impressions from our exchanges. Once I've gotten to know the students and perceived some of their needs, I begin forming guided reading groups. Additionally, to learn more about the readers who will be spending a year of their reading life in my classroom, I ask the following types of reading interview questions:

- Do you like to read?

- What do you usually choose to read?

- What are you reading now?

- What's the name of the last book you read?

- What do you do when you don't know a word when you're reading?

- What do you do if you don't understand what you've read?

The notes I take guide my interventions for individual readers. Moreover, they help me as I develop plans and goals and organize the initial groups for guided reading.

Share Time

At the end of the workshop, bring students back to the central meeting area for approximately five to seven minutes to share their new insights or discoveries. If students have been working on the skill or strategy taught during the day's mini-lesson, they can talk about how they incorporated that idea or topic into their reading work. If students have been working in guided reading groups or individual conferences on a skill or strategy unrelated to the specific mini-lesson taught that day, they can also share a written response to something they read or to a genre, author, or style of writing they're meeting in a text for the first time.

Early in the school year, share time is a good time to reflect on the way the workshop runs. For example, it may include a discussion about important information regarding procedures and setting goals for time spent reading or about student selection of reading materials and ways students record what they read.

Build Stamina for Reading Time

To build stamina for reading time in the beginning, some teachers set a specific amount of time for independent reading. They chart the length of time the reading workshop went well and students stayed focused. They then use that information to decide if they can set a new goal and add another minute or two to the reading time. A corresponding task that can help build reading stamina can be assigned as homework: Have students chart how long they read each night and let them set their own time for extending the duration.

Invite students to share how they maintain focus across the reading of a book and what they do when they lose focus. List ideas on a class chart and add to it as students discover new strategies they find helpful. Share some of the strategies you use to stay focused as well.

Although your role in the share session remains consistent—to guide students to act in ways that will help them as readers—there are quite a few different procedures and approaches you can use to structure share time. Sometimes you may specifically ask a few students to share with the whole class because you know they have something to say that others can learn from. Alternately, students may show or discuss with a partner what they've done or learned. As a third option, you may do a quick "whip around the circle" if the topic is something all students can easily and promptly respond to.

Here are 12 suggestions for how you may use share time:

1. Invite students to make a positive comment about one another and the time spent working together during reading workshop with questions like the following: *What did you see today that helped you know reading workshop went well? Any compliments? How did you figure that out with one another's help?*

2. Ask students to share the title, the author, and the genre of the book they are reading.

3. Have students turn and talk to a partner about something they learned or that happened in the book they read during workshop time.

4. Ask students to tell something they noticed most recently about themselves as a reader, something that surprised them, or something they are proud of.

5. Recommend or advertise a few "good reads" to the class and/or enlist students to share their recommendations.

6. Have students demonstrate and/or explain how they made the transition from the mini-lesson to reading.

7. Ask students to demonstrate and/or explain how they used a reading strategy (connecting, questioning, visualizing, inferring, etc.).

8. Enlist students to read great leads, lines, scenes, or dialogue they come across in the texts they are reading.

9. Have students point out words and phrases in books they are currently reading—any that are unusual, new, appealing, or fun to say.

10. Invite students to ask questions they would like to address to the author— especially those not answered in the text.

11. Share observations you made of students' "brilliance" during reading workshop.

12. Ask students to share something brilliant they did as a reader today.

So, What Are the Other Students Doing?

When establishing routines and procedures, it's important that students know what they are expected to do while you are working with a guided reading group or holding individual conferences. Students who are not in a reading group or reading conference spend most of the workshop period silently reading a self-selected or guided reading text. But remember that it takes time to establish routines, so be sure to model and be clear about what students are expected to do. Monitor students, especially in the beginning of the year, to be sure they are following the established routines and procedures. During reading workshop, students may be doing some of the following:

- reading self-selected texts from the classroom or school library
- reading bookmarked Web sites related to the content areas of study
- reading their guided reading texts you have selected
- partner reading
- listening to and following along with books on audiotape or CD
- writing a response to something they've read
- recording the books they've read in their reading logs
- writing book recommendations or book reviews or critiques
- working on a strategy sheet or extension activity related to the guided reading lesson
- doing research on a topic of their own choosing

Things that students should *not* be doing during the reading portion of the workshop include the following:

- spending the bulk of their time completing worksheets or answering a series of questions
- spending large portions of their time working at literacy centers completing isolated or unrelated activities

- spending long periods of time looking up all the words that are new in a dictionary and writing definitions

Remember, unless students are working directly with you in a guided reading lesson or a reading conference, reading workshop is when students spend the bulk of their time *reading*.

Evaluating Your Reading Workshop

As with just about everything to do with teaching, it's a good idea to periodically evaluate how things are going. In order to examine your reading workshop, you might ask yourself the following questions:

- Does the workshop occupy a predictable, regularly scheduled hour each day?

- Is the transition into reading workshop quick and efficient?

- Is there a dependable structure with clear, consistent procedures in place for each component of the workshop?

- How will I demonstrate or model expected routines and procedures?

- Do students practice the routines and procedures so well that I am free to teach the readers in the class what they need to know?

- If the students run into a problem when I'm not available, do they know how to handle it?

- What materials and texts do students select from?

- Do students know how to self-select a just-right book so their reading time is well spent?

- What do students do if they finish reading a book or selection?

- How do students keep a record of what they've read?

- Are students' options and limits clear and concise enough that they are able to articulate them to me and one another?

- Do students engage in longer blocks of reading so they can really get involved in a book and build reading stamina along with strategies and skills?

IN THE CLASSROOM

Reading Workshop

Fourth-grade teacher Liz Cummings shares some of her thoughts on getting reading workshop started. "I like the beginning of the school year because it's my first chance to get to know the readers in my classroom. It usually takes me about four weeks to launch reading workshop. During those first four weeks, the workshop time looks different than when it's up and running. We usually

(continued on next page)

---

begin the year by talking about our reading identities—who we each are as readers. On the second day of school, I come with a favorite magazine, my latest cookbook with the new recipe I'm trying, my current professional book, and the novel I'm reading. Because reading goes beyond 'books,' I purposely bring in a range of reading materials. By modeling my reading identity, I offer students a glimpse of who I am as a reader and how readers live in the real world.

"In the beginning, it's important that I make myself more available to students until they have a clear understanding of the routines, expectations, and their role during reading workshop. That means I don't start meeting with guided reading groups right away. Before grouping kids, I need to find out just where they are as readers. The first 20 or so days I spend launching reading workshop. I use it not only as a time to get those routines in place but as a chance to observe, confer with, and assess individual students. I use the large block of time in the workshop to start gathering assessment information. I sit right next to a student and talk to him about reading. It's really more like a reading interview where I ask questions to gain insights and information on his attitude, strategies, and goals in reading. I ask the student to read a small portion of a self-selected text he can read pretty well. While he reads, I record errors, self-corrections, reading behaviors, and how the reading sounds—whether it's phrased and fluent. Then I ask the student to tell me about the part he just read, and I take notes as he speaks. I may ask a few follow-up questions to clarify his understanding of an event, information, or vocabulary. In addition, I might use a more formal assessment, like the upper-grade *Developmental Reading Assessment*, if a student is new to the school or if I decide I need additional information on a particular student. My reading assessments are relatively informal but packed with good, usable information

(continued on next page)

TIPS AND TECHNIQUES

Students Talk About Themselves

Early in the year, invite your students to talk about themselves as readers. Have them bring in their favorite books, magazines, collectible cards, and even printed text from favorite Web sites. Or have them visit the school library to find and check out the kinds of things they like to read. Taking time to find out and talk about what students like to read, where and when they read, and the advice they have for other readers gives you a lot of good information about the students in your class. And, it's a great way for students to get to know one another and begin to build a sense of community.

Here are some ways to get students to think and talk about themselves as readers. Have students

- talk about the kinds of books or texts they read.

- talk about their favorite authors/topics.

- share what they're currently reading.

- share when and why they read.

- describe how they go about talking about or recommending a book to others.

- tell what they plan to read next.

- describe what's easy and hard for them as readers.

that I analyze and reflect on in order to determine how to initially group students for guided reading.

"I look at all three components of the reading workshop—the mini-lesson, reading time, and share time—as places to teach and learn more about the readers in my room. Even the share time can be a time for teaching. For example, when I noticed one of my fourth-grade students check out the cover of a book, read the blurb on the back, and then open it up to read the beginning of it, I knew it was important for this student to share with other readers how she previewed and sampled a book as she decided whether or not she wanted to read it.

"Once the students are working productively and I can see evidence of engagement, reading activity, and persistence during the workshop time, I know I can plan to add the small-group guided reading component. It has been my experience that when I give the time to assessing and getting to know the readers in my classroom and establishing predictable workshop routines, I'll be able to work productively with small groups of students while others in the classroom carry on with initiative, purpose, and independence."

The two charts below show how the teaching approaches during reading workshop change for Liz Cummings.

The First Four Weeks of Reading Workshop

During the first four weeks of school, workshop time is spent establishing routines and procedures, gathering assessments, and conferring with individual students.

Mini-Lesson (10–15 minutes)

Routines and procedures

Shared reading or read-aloud

Reading Time (35–45 minutes)

Liz establishes routines/gathers assessments/holds individual reading conferences

Students silently read self-selected texts from book boxes/bags.

Share Time (5–7 minutes)

Group share/evaluation/teach

Reading Workshop After Four Weeks

Once students can work productively on their own and reading assessments have been gathered and analyzed, small-group guided reading can be determined and started.

Mini-Lesson (10–15 minutes)

Shared reading or read-aloud

Reading Time (35–45 minutes)

Liz meets one guided reading group for 15–20 minutes and holds individual reading conferences for the remaining 20–25 minutes

or

(continued on next page)

She meets with two guided reading groups 15–20 minutes each

      or

She holds individual reading conferences, each about 3–7 minutes long, allowing her to confer with five to eight students during the reading portion of the workshop.

Other students silently read self-selected texts from book boxes/bags or guided reading texts.

Share Time (5–7 minutes)

Group share/evaluation/teach

Other Classroom Resources That Support Teaching and Learning

Well-stocked classroom libraries and school book rooms support students and teachers as they engage in reading throughout a comprehensive literacy framework by providing a range of reading material, genres, and content topics.

The Classroom Library

High-quality classroom libraries are a literacy necessity if we expect teaching and learning to happen in our classrooms. Adequate classroom libraries must become a top priority if our students are expected to be actively engaged readers. We cannot teach students about appropriate book selection if there are too few books in the classroom library from which to choose. How does *your* classroom library stand up?

- Do students have access to a large number of quality books and reading materials?

- Is there a range of genres available?

- Is the library organized in clear categories with explicitly labeled bins or baskets?

- Are some of the books at, above, and below the grade level you teach to meet the wide range of readers in your room?

Be selective about the books you choose for your classroom library. The quality and the relevance of the content of books should take precedence over quantity. In addition, books can be moved in and out to reflect the changes in the work the students are doing. For example, when his fourth graders were studying space, Dak Smith made sure that all relevant books were prominently featured in the library. Be sure to include material other than books, such as selected brochures, posters, sports pages or kids' sections from magazines and newspapers, catalogs, Internet articles, students' writing, teachers' writing, maps, charts, graphs, travel timetables, and magazine and newspaper advertisements.

Sources for Books

Book sources for classroom libraries might include the following:

- Book vendors (see Appendix)
- Library closeouts
- Grants targeting book acquisition
- Yard sales
- Book clubs and club points
- Book warehouse sales
- Online bookstores
- Donations made by parents and/or students
- Parent Teacher Association contributions

IN THE CLASSROOM

Organizing a Classroom Library

During the first two weeks of school, Jennifer Orr's fourth-grade students help organize 500-plus books for the classroom library. To help her class become familiar with the books, Jennifer includes students in the library's organization right from the start. They begin by discussing and making a list of possible ways to organize the

books. Initially, everyone works together looking at, talking about, and deciding on ways to sort the books into categories. As books are categorized, they're placed in baskets for easy access. The baskets are then labeled with 4-by-6-inch index cards that students have decorated. The labels designate the type of books in each basket.

Jennifer says that involving the students has really made a difference. She explains, "Since I've begun including students in organizing the classroom library, I've noticed that they have a much better idea of the reading materials on the shelves. They're actually picking up books to read that have rarely been selected by students in the past. I've come to realize how important it is for students to know firsthand what's here for them to read, and since they're a part of the selection process, they're really aware of what's here."

TIPS AND TECHNIQUES

"Advertising" Books

Give a book talk or read short, powerful excerpts from picture books, novels, nonfiction trade books, and magazines to recommend or "advertise" them so students are enticed to select them for independent reading. Teacher Lisa Washington says she is amazed at how many students will run to check out the books that she advertises in this way. Sometimes it may be something as simple as the teacher recommending the book that hooks a reluctant reader.

The book room at London Towne Elementary School is centrally located and serves as a place to house sets of guided reading books for schoolwide use. Many books are color-coded and organized by literacy levels in plastic bins.

School Book Rooms

In most schools, the book room is centrally located and serves as a place to house sets of guided reading books, novel sets or series books, shared reading Big Books, and small sets of books with audiocassette tapes for schoolwide use. Some book rooms also include a place where multiple copies of magazines or newspapers are available for guided reading use. For example, multiple subscriptions of *Scholastic News*, *Kids Discover*, and *National Geographic* are good sources for short pieces to use for guided reading. (See Appendix for a list of periodical/ book sources.)

> *K*ids not only need to read a lot but they also need lots of books they can read right at their fingertips. They also need access to books that entice them, attract them to reading. Schools can foster wider reading by creating school and classroom collections that provide a rich and wide array of appropriate books and magazines and by providing time every day for children to actually sit and read.
>
> —Richard Allington,
> *What Really Matters for Struggling Readers*

Selections should include a range of levels and text types or genres. You will want to create a system for organizing some of the guided reading books in a sequence or continuum of text difficulty so teachers can easily reach for the appropriate book level for specific readers. A continuum of text difficulty is an ordering or ranking of

This third-grade ELL student listens to a book on tape.

books according to a specific set of criteria or characteristics. As you move along the continuum, the texts are ordered from easier to more challenging or complex. There are several variations of these criteria for leveling books. Not every book should or needs to be leveled. Books may also be arranged by text type to facilitate the study of a particular form or genre. For example, all biographies or poetry selections may be arranged in an area together in the book room.

Final Thoughts

By establishing reading workshop routines at the outset, helping guide students to self-select just-right texts for independent reading, and gathering assessment information on the readers in your room, you put in place the essentials that will make it possible for you to work with students in guided reading groups and individual reading conferences. Remember that although you will not include guided reading in your reading workshop at the start of the year, you will be teaching reading from day one. The mini-lessons you teach, which incorporate either shared reading or a read-aloud, give you time for direct instruction. And while students are reading independently, you will be available to hold individual reading conferences. Not only are individual conferences a perfect place to learn more about the strengths and needs of each reader in your classroom, but they also provide an ideal chance to tailor reading instruction for each student. And don't forget the share time at the end of the workshop. Fine-tune your share time by using your observations of what students are doing as readers during the rest of workshop. And remember that share time is a time to teach, too.

Once you have a clear understanding of what students know and can do as readers, you can begin forming guided reading groups to use your reading workshop time most effectively and efficiently. One added benefit of small-group guided reading groups is that they provide opportunities for students to learn from others' thinking, knowledge, and responses to commonly read texts.

In Chapter 6, I describe four guided reading lessons. For each lesson I show you the specific student need, the lesson focus, how the teaching is connected to previous learning, and how the lesson takes shape before, during, and after reading.

Chapter 6

Jessica Howell and a group of sixth-grade students discuss a guided reading nonfiction text selection after reading.

Putting It Into Practice: Four Model Guided Reading Lessons

The craft of teaching is inextricably tied to the craft of listening to our kids and acting on what they tell us.

—Linda Rief and Maureen Barbieri, *All That Matters*

In this chapter, I take you into intermediate classrooms where guided reading instruction takes place in small, flexible groups during reading workshop—part of a comprehensive framework that includes read-alouds, shared reading, literature study groups, partner reading, and independent reading.

I mention again the components available to teach reading because each of the four guided reading lessons that follows is built on the foundation of the strategy instruction that has already taken place in read-alouds and shared reading with the students. Therefore, none of the guided reading lessons you'll see here are introducing strategies or types of text for the first time.

In the opening two lessons, students encounter nonfiction texts. The first lesson involves students who rarely preview a text before reading on their own. The guided reading lesson focuses on the importance of preparing before beginning to read by activating prior knowledge. The second lesson focuses on using key words to summarize. In the final two guided reading lessons, students read two fiction selections—a trickster tale and an excerpt from a historical novel. The third lesson, which was part of an ongoing genre study of folktales, focuses on giving students experience reading a trickster tale and building a more extensive understanding of the characteristics of different kinds of folktales. The fourth lesson focuses on understanding point of view and perspective, through questioning and inferring, in an excerpt from a historical fiction novel.

How the Guided Reading Lessons Are Organized

The lessons in this chapter address an important aspect of reading comprehension for each of the guided reading groups. You'll notice that the lessons have been organized within the following framework:

- **Materials.** Each lesson starts with a list of the key materials you will need to conduct the lesson.

- **What I Noticed.** At the beginning of each lesson I include a description of an area I've noticed students need more practice in. The "noticing" comes from my ongoing assessment and work alongside students throughout reading workshop.

- **Focus.** The guided reading lesson focus comes directly from what I've noticed and observed students need to learn. It has been decided before the lesson begins and is entirely directed by student need. I explicitly state the focus so students know what will be taught in the guided reading lesson that day.

- **Connect to Previous Lessons.** The focus is often set in the context of students' ongoing reading work by picking up the thread of what we did in our read-aloud, shared reading, or last guided reading lesson. Each guided reading lesson builds on our prior work. Having a real sense of the focus and the previous reading work we've done helps me select a guided reading text for the lesson. I read the selection ahead of time so I know what will support the readers but still provide a few challenges.

- **Before Reading: Tune In to the Text.** Before reading I help students get ready to read by actively thinking about and relating to the text they are about to read. It's an opportunity to get students thinking about the content, concepts, or information that will support the reading of the text, and it creates an atmosphere for discussion and thinking before reading. Tuning in may include some of the following activities:
  - connecting to what they already know about the content
  - previewing the text (title, headings, captions)
  - discussing vocabulary and concepts central to the text/topic

- reading a short portion of the text to build knowledge (introduction, captions, chart)

- skimming or scanning the text quickly to gather bits of information

- writing to discover and explore thinking

- talking and listening to one another's thinking about the text

When planning for the before-reading part of the lesson, I consider the types of engagement and interaction that will support the focus and best activate background knowledge so students can undertake the reading successfully.

- **During Reading: Students Read the Text.** Students read individually and silently their own copy of the same text. At times, they may mark, code, or record their thinking on the text or on sticky-notes. Jotting down information helps students to think as they read. Readers are far more likely to remember information if they jot something down, highlight, or code as they go. This is especially true when reading nonfiction because it's not unusual to encounter large amounts of new information.

  When students are reading, it's a good time for me to observe their reading behaviors and jot down anecdotal notes. Sometimes I take a record of oral reading on a couple of students and ask them to talk briefly about what they are reading and learning. By using this time to notice the kinds of strategic actions readers use and considering how and why they use them, I am better able to support them. I may teach on the spot or use what I've learned to help plan the next guided reading lesson.

- **After Reading: Return to the Focus and Dig Deeper.** After reading we usually revisit the focus and purpose for reading as we begin our discussion. It's also an ideal time to provoke thought through discussion to help students clarify and extend their thinking about the text. It is very important to revisit the text to provide evidence of the ideas and understandings that we discussed before the reading commenced. Not only do I bring the discussion back into the text, I find that our talk purposely takes the students beyond the text. We do not just talk about what they read; we talk about what it means and how the reading connects to their world beyond the classroom walls.

- **Observations About the Lesson and Lesson Follow-Up.** At the end of a lesson it's always important to step back and reflect on what worked, what students learned, and what learning goals still remain. It's also valuable to informally map out follow-up instruction and/or signs you will be watching for in students' ongoing reading behaviors.

  Of course, the intention is for students to successfully use the strategies they already know how to use as well as the strategy that we are focusing on in guided reading, but our goal goes beyond the text we are using in each of these particular guided reading lessons. Ultimately, we are teaching and helping develop a repertoire of strategies students can actively apply to *all* reading, most of all to what they read independently.

Note: Each of the following lessons is based on a sample text that can be found in the Appendix of this book.

✳

Guided Reading Lesson 1:
Previewing to Activate Background Knowledge

Materials

"Great Gliders" by Tim Laman (page 154), chart paper, markers, sticky-notes, markers

What I Noticed

During individual reading conferences, I noticed that Sam, Keesha, Lucas, Hinda, and Jesse continually rushed into reading without taking any time before beginning to think about what they might encounter in the text. As I conferred with them, I found that they were unable to tell how they got ready to read or what they thought about or did to preview a text. They often had difficulty talking about what they read and how it connected to what they already knew. In the midst of a reading conference Lucas remarked, "Oh, I forgot, I'm supposed to think about what might happen when I start to read."

Focus

As a result of my observations and discussions, I realized that I had to plan some guided reading lessons to give this group of students multiple opportunities to think about what they already knew about a topic before getting into a text. I needed to help them preview to activate their prior knowledge and use it to think about what they were about to read. I also wanted them to be able to discuss how thinking about what they already knew actually helped them understand what they read.

Connect to Previous Lessons

For these five third-grade students, I selected the short informational text "Great Gliders" by Tim Laman. This descriptive text about nocturnal animals of the rain forest includes text features such as a title, headings, sequenced photographs, boldface print, labels, word definitions, and signal words such as *first, then,* and *once.* When students are working on a strategy, I usually select a text students can read with relative ease. That way their attention isn't focused on word solving but is instead directed toward a particular strategy and how to use it in relation to the text.

Additionally, because the rain forest is a topic the students are familiar with from their science curriculum, I wanted these students to call on existing knowledge before they began reading the text. Using a familiar topic helps support my attempts to focus students' attention on what they already know and build understanding before they begin reading. Because they have to do only minimal word-solving work on the text, their attention is focused on connecting their prior knowledge to what they are reading.

Before Reading: Tune In to the Text (approximately 6 minutes)

Prior to reading the text, I began the guided reading lesson with a word prediction to engage the students in vocabulary and meaning exploration. The purpose of a word prediction is to get students to think ahead of time about the topic-related vocabulary they might encounter. It also serves as a way to get students who are "under-predictive" readers to actively discuss possibilities about the content and genre (Hoyt, 2000).

Lesson Dialogue	Notes
Readers, we've talked about ways to get ready to read. You can read the title and the author's name, check out illustrations on the front cover, and even read the blurb on the back. Yesterday, when we did a shared reading of the nonfiction article on the rain forest in science, we got ready to read by doing some similar things. We read the title, looked at the photographs and captions, and read the headings. Then you talked to a partner about what you expected to read and find out from the article.	I remind students of some of the ways readers get ready to read. By reminding students of what they have already learned, I am building on previous lessons they've encountered. In addition, I need to make sure they recognize that readers monitor their predictions throughout a text. As they continually revise predictions, new ones are generated, which in turn support the construction of new meaning. I could have asked the students all the different ways we have learned to get ready to read. But questioning the students to elicit their answers at the beginning of the lesson would take time away from the focus of the lesson: previewing and thinking about what they already know before reading the text. Sometimes it's important to just come right out and tell the students what we've been learning and talking about as readers.
Readers, it's important that you think about what you know and what you might learn before reading. That way, you can connect what you already know to what you read. And it's important to do it whether we're reading together or you're reading on your own.	Notice that I want students to understand why thinking about what they know before reading is important. I also want them to be aware that it's important to do this whenever they're reading. *(continued on next page)*

Lesson Dialogue	Notes
*Today I want you to work on something I hope you will all do whenever you're getting ready to read. Whenever you get ready to read, you should **look, think**, and **predict** before reading. That means you just don't pick up a book or article and start reading. Instead, it means you look at, or preview, the book or article before you start reading. You think to yourself: What do I already know about this? Then you try to answer that question. The reason we're doing this is because it will help you better understand what you're reading. That way, when you're reading you can check your predictions against what you're reading to see if you're right or if you have to change them.*	I make my instruction explicit so students know what they will be learning or working on in this lesson. I give them a kind of routine—*look, think, predict*—as a way to put "getting ready to read" into practice. Over time, I shift from saying "look at the text" to "preview the text."
*Let's give it a try with the article "Great Gliders" by Tim Laman. Remember, I don't want you to read it just yet. I want you to look at as much of the article as you can very quickly. **Skim** it to see what information you can pick up from checking out the title, author, photographs, labels, and headings. **Think** about what might be in this article. **Predict** what words or information might be found in the reading. Then we'll talk about what you've noticed and your predictions. (Students begin to preview text on their own.)*	I give students explicit directions about what they are to do with the article before reading. Because this is an informational text, I want students to realize that they need to gather and select information from a number of sources—title, author blurb, photographs, labels, and headings. I keep the time short, approximately 60–90 seconds, because I don't want students to actually begin reading the text. I want to give them just enough time to sample some of the text features to get a general idea of what the selection is about. Then we can move into our discussion of what they noticed and start our word prediction list.
Now that you've had a chance to quickly look at "Great Gliders," let's talk about the words and information you either noticed or think might be found in the article. We'll quickly go around the table a few times so each of you can tell us the word or words you expect to find in the reading. Also, make sure you tell us how you came up with the word—what was your thinking? I will jot the words down on the chart. *Hinda responds first. She says, I think the words* flying lemur *and* wings *will be in it. I noticed how it is labeled in the picture, and it has its wings wide open in another picture as it's flying.*	When students generate a list of words while previewing the text and predict what might be found in the reading, they are activating prior knowledge and using it to think about what they are about to read. This activity also sparks vocabulary building and meaning exploration. I list the words and ideas on chart paper so we can refer to them after reading the selection. It's important for the students to understand that readers confirm or revise predictions as they read.
*So, Hinda, you're using what you noticed about the labeled photograph and you're predicting another word—*wings—*based on what was happening in the second photograph and what you know about animals that fly.*	Notice how I restate for Hinda what she did as a reader, which includes using information she picked up from previewing the text as well as making a prediction based on that information and what she already knew about animals that fly.

During Reading: Students Read the Text
(approximately 5 minutes)

During the reading the students need to actively engage and interact with the text to bring relevant experiences and knowledge to mind. Setting a purpose for reading this particular text alerts them to what they should turn their attention to when reading.

Lesson Dialogue	Notes
Now that you've generated a list of words you might meet in the text, it's time for you to read "Great Gliders" on your own. As you read, think about why the author thinks these animals are great gliders. Also, see if you notice any of the words on our list. Remember to jot down any tricky words you can't work out or don't know the meaning of on your sticky-note. We'll talk about them after we read. If you finish early, go back to the article and reread to search for words from our chart. Use your marker to underline them. I'll be asking a few of you to read or to talk about what you're finding out about these great gliders so far. (Students begin to silently read their copies of "Great Gliders.")	I give students a purpose for reading the text. I often jot the purpose on a whiteboard so students can refer back to it while reading. After reading, our discussion typically leads with our purpose for reading. Because the selected text is well within students' level of reading, I decide to have them read it in its entirety. I encourage students to think about the list of words we generated together to bring meaning to the text as they read. I give them the responsibility of monitoring their reading by keeping track of difficult or unknown words. Because students read at different rates, I plan for early finishers to go back into the text to search for and locate words from the prediction list. I usually use the time students are reading to gather some assessment information. Sometimes I select one or two students to read aloud a portion of the text and record oral reading behaviors. Or I may ask one or two students to briefly talk about what they're learning from the selection. I bring any information I've gathered that may benefit the group into our after-reading discussion.

After Reading: Return to the Focus and Dig Deeper (approximately 9 minutes)

After reading, we began the discussion by talking about the purpose for reading—why the author thinks these animals are great gliders. As the students shared what they learned, they made connections between what they already knew and information that they picked up from the text. The students returned to the text, citing information that supported their statements and thoughts. We then discussed our deeper understanding of concepts and the content and wondered aloud about some additional questions about animals that glide in the rain forest. We talked about where we might find that information. Eventually, our discussion led us to pose additional questions we would ask Tim Laman, the author, if we had the chance. We talked about what we still wanted to know. Before ending, I brought the students' attention back to the word prediction chart so we could check and confirm which predicted words actually showed up in the passage. Revisiting the chart demonstrated for the students how taking the time to get ready to read helps support our understanding of the text. We also discovered that some of our words on the chart were synonyms for words the author used in the text.

Mary and third-grade students during the after reading discussion of the passage "Great Gliders." The word prediction chart was generated before students read the selection. Notice that it's not an exhaustive list of words, but rather serves as an active and constructive way to help students make meaning before reading and later after reading when revisiting the chart.

Observations About the Lesson and Lesson Follow-Up

The prior knowledge that students bring to reading can greatly influence their understanding of the text. Showing students how to make connections to prior knowledge directs their attention to what they already know and prepares them for some of the ideas they will encounter in the text. Over the next few weeks, the students in this guided reading group continued to meet so they could practice taking more conscious action in activating their prior knowledge before reading, seeing how doing so supported their understanding of the text. During individual reading conferences, the classroom teacher and I also discussed with students how they were applying what they were learning about previewing and thinking about what they already knew to get ready to read and how that added to their understanding.

This lesson revealed to these five students how we can relate to the text through preparation and use of our existing knowledge. It also demonstrated to the students how we contributed to our new knowledge and understanding by sharing what we think, by responding to one another's observations, and by analyzing the text before, during, and after reading.

TIPS AND TECHNIQUES

Anticipation Guides

An anticipation guide is used to activate and assess students' knowledge before reading. It helps readers to make predictions and think about what they know through previous experiences, to make educated guesses about the material to be read. An anticipation guide usually has a series of short, declarative statements. Students respond to the statements and discuss their predictions and anticipatory ideas prior to reading the text selection. Then students read the text. After reading, students return to the anticipation guide and discuss and evaluate the statements in light of the author's intent and their own interpretations. An anticipation guide is a technique that can be used in all subject areas prior to reading a passage, article, poem, or chapter.

Here is an example of an anticipation guide one student completed before and after reading the text passage "Kids Need More Zzzs," found in the Appendix.

Do you agree (A) or disagree (D) with the statement?

Before (ME)	Text (Author)	Statement	Reaction
D	A	Kids don't get enough sleep.	I do but other kids might not get enough sleep!
D	A	Kids who have TVs in their bedrooms go to sleep later than kids without TVs in their rooms.	I watch 2X. Mine at night before bed but some people spend hrs of t, v
A	A	Caffeine can keep you awake.	I would definitely agree!
A	A	Too little sleep can keep you from learning.	Yeah, look at the picture!
D	D 10 -11	Fifth grade students need about 7 or 8 hours of sleep.	She said 10-11 hours as needed. I said the same.

Name___Alexander___

Nonfiction Text Features
and Structures

Help students learn to pay attention to and use the various nonfiction text features and structures that alert readers to important information. Nonfiction texts can be infused into the curriculum throughout the day's teaching with learners at all levels. Use nonfiction Big Books or short pieces of lifted texts to introduce students to and familiarize them with the various text structures and features during shared reading. Later on, reacquaint students with them during guided reading instruction. These text features may include the following:

Nonfiction Text Features		What Students Need to Learn and Know
Font and Special-Effect Print Features	Titles Headings/subheadings Boldface, colored, or italicized print Bullets or numbers Captions Labels	• How to quickly and efficiently use various text organizers, headings, and subheadings to gather information and make decisions about what to read • Why authors use fonts and special effects such as boldface, colored, and italicized print to highlight text
Text Organizers	Table of contents Preface Index Glossary Pronunciation guide Appendix	• How to examine, interpret, and integrate information from visual graphics, captions, labels, illustrations, and photographs with the written text
Visual Graphics	Illustrations Photographs Drawings Paintings Graphs Diagrams Charts Tables Cutaways Cross sections Maps	• How to examine for detail, infer, and connect visual graphics, captions, labels, illustrations, and photographs with the written text *(continued on next page)*

Nonfiction Text Features		What Students Need to Learn and Know
Textual cues	Verbal cues or signal words help the reader to understand how the information is organized and what is important. • Continuation signals (*and, also, again, another, in addition, next*) • Change-of-direction signals (*however, while, but, instead, still, different from, in contrast, yet*) • Sequence signals (*first, second, third, then, next, last, before, after, finally*) • Illustration signals (*for example, such as, similar to, for instance, to illustrate, specifically, much like*) • Cause or result signals (*because, so that, then, therefore, consequently*)	• How the words the author uses signal how information is organized and provide clues to what is important • How to recognize and use signal words to predict and confirm • How to identify and analyze the text structure to provide clues to how information is organized and what is important • How the author's purpose and the subject matter affect the various structures • Why authors choose to convey particular information through various text structures • Which language and syntactical structures often identify the various text structures

Here are six of the most common nonfiction text structures. These examples are typical of how nonfiction text is structured. All the sentences have been built around the concept of *stage fright*.

Cause and effect. Speaking in front of a group gives me stage fright. I get butterflies in my stomach and I start to sweat. (Gives reasons or explanations for happenings.)

Problem and solution. Stage fright makes me fearful of public speaking. Practicing my material and presentation makes me confident and relieves my stage fright. (States a problem and its solution.)

Question and answer. What happens to some people when they have to speak in front of a group? They get stage fright. (Asks a question and answers it.)

Comparison and contrast. Some people have stage fright speaking in front of a group, while others do it effortlessly and without worry. (Looks at two or more items to establish similarities and differences.)

Description. Stage fright makes it difficult for me to speak in front of groups. I start to sweat and it feels like I have butterflies in my stomach. (Describes details of characteristics, actions, opinions, etc.)

Sequence (time/order). Right before I have to speak in front of a group I start to get nervous. My stomach turns upside down, and pretty soon I begin to sweat all over. (Gives information in order of occurrence.)

Guided Reading Lesson 2:
Using Key Words to Summarize

Materials

"Oceans in Danger: Marine Wildlife Is Disappearing," by Barry Rust (page 141), markers, sticky-notes

What I Noticed

During shared reading lessons, fourth graders were gaining control over reading and summarizing short portions of nonfiction texts to better understand what they read. Together, we read fairly short segments of text. We then stopped to identify a key word or phrase that summarized each segment. As we worked through various texts together over the course of a couple of weeks, I noticed many of the students were successfully choosing between more important and less important information as they read. Sometimes their words came directly from the text, and sometimes they were a combination of the text and their response to it. In addition, the students could support why they chose a particular key word or phrase to summarize their thinking about that part of the text. Because students were demonstrating their understanding of summarizing in shared reading texts, I decided it was time to ask them to apply their learning about summarizing texts to support understanding in guided reading.

Focus

Rather than have the students read a piece in its entirety, I asked students to read a short section on their own and then stop and identify a key word or phrase that summarized the segment that they'd just read. Using key words to summarize helps students monitor their understanding and determine the most important facts or ideas as they read. It is important that students explain how and why they decided on a particular key word or phrase. This technique is especially helpful with content-related texts.

Connect to Previous Lessons

To help students practice summarizing a short nonfiction selection on their own, I chose the article "Oceans in Danger: Marine Wildlife Is Disappearing." This article dovetailed with familiar science curriculum topics involving oceans and ocean life. This short expository text reports the problem of overfishing, its causes and effects, and possible solutions. Some text features include title, subtitle, photograph, caption, expert testimony, and a Web site for further reading. Of course, this guided reading lesson sits squarely on the shoulders of the shared reading lessons in which students engaged in identifying key words or phrases to summarize with more of my help. This lesson begins the process of shifting responsibility from the teacher to students for summarizing the key ideas in nonfiction text they'll read on their own.

Before Reading: Tune In to the Text
(approximately 7 minutes)

After reading the title of the article and captions under the photograph, our guided reading lesson began with a discussion that centered on the questions *Why do you think ocean life might be in danger?* and *What would cause some animal life to disappear?* We discussed the concept of extinction and listed some reasons why marine animals become endangered. A recap of our lesson follows.

Lesson Dialogue	Notes
Today we're going to read an article about ocean life and possible dangers that exist for some of the wildlife. I want you to think about what you've been learning and the information that you've been reading in science about oceans and ocean life. Thinking about what you already know can add to your understanding of what you read today.	I remind students to reflect back on the reading and learning about ocean life they have been doing in science.
Let's begin by reading the title, subtitle, and caption under the photograph.	Reading the title, subtitle, and caption under the photograph gives students time to begin to activate and apply relevant background knowledge and generate predictions before reading.
Now, think about these two questions: Why do you think ocean life might be in danger? What would cause some animal life to disappear?	As students respond to the questions, I write their ideas on a chart. Capturing students' thinking before they begin reading helps them to consider key ideas and concepts ahead of time. Having a record of their thinking makes it easy to go back later to confirm, clarify, revise, or add to our understandings. It also serves as a place to record and sort out the meaning of specialized vocabulary used in the text and/or discussion.
Readers, now that we've listed some reasons why marine animals might become endangered, it's time for you to do some reading on your own to see if our ideas match some of what the author says in this article. We'll come back to the chart after you read to check, confirm, or revise our thinking.	I want students to know that the thinking and discussion we have before reading is relevant to the topic of the text they will read. Returning to the chart later helps students realize that the meaning readers initially anticipated needs to be confirmed, clarified, or revised.
*As you read this article today, I want you to use the **key word strategy** to summarize your thinking as you read. Remember how you practiced the key word strategy with a partner during shared reading? You read a short bit, stopped, thought, and then wrote on a sticky-note a word or phrase that you and your partner thought was especially important.*	Here I am telling students what strategy they will be using as they read the article. I remind them of the previous lessons in which they used the key word strategy with a partner. I review the sequence of the key word strategy.

(continued on next page)

Lesson Dialogue	Notes
Today, I want you to try using the **key word strategy** as you read on your own to summarize your thinking about the article "Oceans in Danger: Marine Wildlife Is Disappearing." Before I ask you to do it, though, I am going to think aloud to show you how I would go about deciding on the key word or phrase for the first paragraph. Watch me so you can then try it.	Even though students have practiced the key word strategy already, I want to provide a demonstration with this article so they can readily draw on it when they read. This is one more step in that gradual release of responsibility before I ask students to decide on their own which word or phrase summarizes their understanding.

During Reading: Students Read the Text (approximately 7 minutes)

Because this was the first time students were going to summarize and identify key words and phrases on their own, I walked them through the process first by thinking aloud as I read and summarized the first paragraph. The students read the next three paragraphs and summarized their thinking before we stopped to talk about which key words they selected and why.

Lesson Dialogue	Notes
(I begin by reading aloud the first paragraph of the article.) *"Earlier this year, a group of scientists finished a 10-year project to count tuna, cod, swordfish, and other large fish in the world's oceans."* Hmm, okay, scientists have spent 10 years on a project counting large fish. I'm wondering how they do that and why they do that. It seems like a long time to me. Reading on may tell me."	The think-aloud technique is a clear way to demonstrate that readers think about *what* they read *while* they read. As I read the first paragraph, I stop and say out loud what I'm specifically thinking inside my head in order to make sense of the text. Showing students the thought processes I use to construct meaning makes the reading process more visible and models the inner conversations readers have while reading. Notice how I wonder about what I've read. It shows students that readers ask questions even with relatively small amounts of text.
(I read on to the end of the paragraph.) *"They made a shocking discovery: These fish are almost gone."* Okay, so it tells me what scientists found out, but not exactly how and why they did it. That information may come later in the article.	Here I stop to rephrase in my own words what the article is telling me so far. Notice how I'm still aware that I have other questions and, as a reader, anticipate they might be answered later in the reading.
So, let's see, what would be a key word or phrase that would describe the big idea of this paragraph? Hmm, I'd have to say discovery, because that's what happened at the end of the 10-year project. Scientists made a "discovery," or	Here I come back to my purpose for reading— to summarize the most important idea of the portion I've read. I ask the question *What would be a key word or phrase that would describe the big idea of this paragraph?* This

(continued on next page)

Lesson Dialogue	Notes
found out, that large ocean fish are almost gone. That could cause some real problems. The author also said it was "shocking," so just from that word, I can infer that this discovery was upsetting and not expected. I can see how it would be shocking to find out that most of the big fish are disappearing. Ahh, disappearing—that's in the title, 'Marine Wildlife Is Disappearing'. Okay, I think "shocking discovery" can be my key words because it summarizes my understanding about this paragraph and it will help me remember the shocking or upsetting information scientists found out about the larger fish in the ocean disappearing. So I'll write "shocking discovery" on this sticky-note and put it next to the first paragraph.	shows how questions can keep the reader engaged and on track. I come up with the key word and then expand on my mental processes behind the selection of that particular word. In my attempt to explain why the word *discovery* would be a good key word, I realize the meaning I'm constructing links right back to the title of the article. Readers need to connect bits of information as they read to construct meaning and to enhance understanding.
Readers, did you hear the thinking I'm doing inside my head as I'm reading? Did you see how it helps me figure out a key word or phrase to summarize what I'm reading?	I am letting students know that it is important that readers think *while* reading and how that thinking helps the reader decide what is important information.
*Readers, did you see how I read a short bit, stopped, did some thinking about what I read, and then identified a key word or phrase that summarizes that portion? Once I decided on my **key words**, I wrote it on a sticky-note and put it next to that paragraph.*	My job during a think-aloud is to demonstrate my thinking processes and the strategic actions I use as a reader. Using the think-aloud technique during shared and guided reading lessons with students is an explicit way to demonstrate how I think about what's most important when I read. I can't just assign the task or tell them to do it, I need to show them how to do it so that when they try it, they will know how to apply the strategy successfully.
Now it's your turn to try out the key word strategy as you read on your own. Read the next three paragraphs. At the end of each paragraph, stop, think, and write a word or phrase that is especially important in the part you read. Then we'll come back together to compare the key words or phrases that summarize the important ideas. Remember, if there are any tricky words you can't work out or don't know the meaning of, jot them down. We'll talk about them after we read. If you finish early, reread the three paragraphs to be sure you can support why you chose a key word or phrase. (Students begin to read individually and silently their own copy of "Oceans in Danger: Marine Wildlife Is Disappearing.")	I recap the sequence of the key word strategy I want students to use as they read the remainder of the article. During shared reading, students summarized text with my guidance and support. Now, in guided reading, I give them a small portion to read and apply the strategy independently. I observe readers in the midst of their reading work to see if they can effectively summarize each paragraph with a key word or phrase.

The Think-Aloud Technique

Teachers use the think-aloud technique to help students understand how they make meaning when they read (Davey, 1983; Wilhelm 2001). The think-aloud is a kind of oral thinking the teacher uses to show students how she constructs meaning and thinks about her reading. Before reading a book or selection aloud, the teacher tells the students that she will be stopping occasionally to say aloud what is actually going through her mind while reading. It might include connections she's making, questions that occur, problems with understanding that she's encountering, and the possible ways she knows how to fix those problems. The think-aloud technique is a clear way to demonstrate that readers think about *what* they read *while* they read. Students may hear statements such as *I think the author included that part because he wants us to think about how we might feel in the same circumstance.* Or, *Hmm, the paragraph I just read has a lot of information in it. I'm not sure I got it all on the first read. I think I should go back to reread it and slow down so I'm sure I get all of what it's telling me.* Or, *When I read those words, the picture in my head was . . .*

Showing students the thought processes readers use to construct meaning makes the reading process more visible and models the inner conversations readers have while reading. Because struggling readers and ELL students often need extra support in structuring these kinds of inner conversations, modeling and using think-alouds can be especially helpful to these learners.

You may want to use the think-aloud technique whenever you're moving from one genre or text form to another. Don't expect that just because you've modeled how you think through one type of text—such as a short informational article—that students will automatically be able to apply it to a poem.

After you've modeled thinking aloud a few times, give students a chance to try it on a short amount of text with a partner. As with any new learning students take on, you probably will have to scaffold their think-aloud attempts. Be specific about how much you want them to read, where you want them to stop, and what you want them to respond to—what they visualized or imagined, a connection they made, or something they wonder about. Remind them that readers think while they read and constantly have a running dialogue in their head and are actively engaged with the reading. You will need to frequently model and practice this technique with the students.

As you can see from the previous think-aloud dialogue, although my purpose was to demonstrate for students how to identify a key word or phrase, it was impossible to read for understanding without employing other strategies at the same time. I monitored as I read, anticipated what would come next, asked questions, determined what information was important to keep and eliminate while reading, made connections, and stopped to summarize. As readers, we always draw on a repertoire of strategies to understand what we read even though here the focus of instruction highlighted only one strategy—summarizing using key words.

After Reading: Return to the Focus and Dig Deeper (approximately 9 minutes)

When students finished reading the next three paragraphs in the text, we discussed how they applied the key word strategy to help them summarize their thinking and broaden their understanding of the content as they read. Students began by sharing the key word or phrase on their sticky-note for the first paragraph they read. Their sticky-note responses included the following key words: *technologies, sound wave technologies, fishing technologies,* and *new fishing technologies.* We compared how some key word summaries were the same and some slightly different, yet they had similar meanings. Next, students recounted some of the thinking processes they used to identify key words or phrases.

For instance, Neehah explained her summary of the third paragraph this way: "After I read the paragraph, I asked myself, What is this mostly about? I decided the best words to summarize this paragraph would be *new fishing technologies*. That's because it gives us examples of these fishing technologies. It says there are things like sonar so they can figure out where the fish are. And they have huge boats that can travel for a long time without refueling. And also, there is the fact that they can catch huge amounts of fish that these big boats can carry." According to Jack, the word *technologies* summarized the third paragraph. He explained, "Well, I started thinking

Sample of passage with student's key words and phrases written on sticky-notes.

I'd use the words *detect fish* to summarize the paragraph, but then I reread the paragraph a second time, and I pictured all these fishermen using all kinds of state-of-the-art equipment and tools—like sonar that gives off sound waves and huge fishing boats—to help them find and catch fish. So then I decided that a better word to summarize it would be *technologies*, because that's what the equipment they describe is."

Observations About the Lesson and Lesson Follow-Up

We can see that Neehah focused her thinking by asking herself a question and then answered it using the key ideas in the paragraph. She successfully linked her knowledge with the purpose for reading. Notice how Jack shifted his thinking after a second reading of the paragraph. He slowed down and reread to clarify his thinking before going on. His explanation illustrated how picturing or visualizing what he read clarified his thinking and led him to revise his key word summary. Based on these descriptions, we can see that Neehah and Jack were able to apply the key word strategy to orally summarize the portion of text they read. When students are aware of their thinking processes, apply strategies in flexible ways, and can explain their processes, they, along with their peers, profit from the diversity of thinking and learning possibilities.

Because students demonstrated a clear understanding of what to do to summarize each paragraph, I asked the students to read the remainder of the article on their own at their desks. We planned to meet again the next day for about 15 minutes to discuss the rest of the article and the key words they'd identified to summarize each remaining paragraph.

Guided Reading Lesson 3:
Reading and Responding to Folktales

Background Note

Folktales, usually narrative in form, are born of the oral traditions and have been passed down through the years. Over time, many folktales have been written down, and variants exist in many cultures. Folktales are perfect for helping students recognize patterns or motifs that recur across tales. Some patterns or common motifs found in folktales that will help students see similar elements across cultures and tales include the following:

- *similar characters, such as the wicked stepmother, the clever trickster, or the giant*

- *magical objects, such as a slipper, a magic pot, or a doll*

- *magical powers given to people or animals*

- *magical transformations, such as an animal into a person or vice versa*

- *enchantments and long sleeps that symbolically represent the coming of winter or death*

- *wishes that are granted and often used foolishly or do not come true without the fulfillment of a task or trial*

- *trickery by animals and people*

When students are exposed to a wide array of stories and structures, they build their under-
standing of the conventions and literary devices that are the cornerstone of folktales.
Additionally, listening to, reading, and talking about folktales can help students understand
the ways of humankind and their world today, the same way folklore explained the world to
people in the past.

Materials

"The Red and Blue Coat: A Trickster Tale from the Congo" (page 142), whiteboard easel or
chart paper, markers

What I Noticed

I began the genre study of folktales by gathering the class of fifth graders to discuss what they
already knew about folktales. I gave students time to turn and talk to a partner to activate their
thinking and prepare possible ideas they could contribute during the whole-group discussion. As
students shared their ideas with the whole group, I listed them on a chart titled "What We Know
About Folktales." I noticed the students mainly discussed what they knew about familiar fairytales
and the events in those stories. Some students were familiar with a few of the variants of the
fairytales that basically told the same story or plot as the original but incorporated different
characters, settings, and motifs.

Later, when I reviewed the chart we'd generated together, I noticed that the students had a
strong general acquaintance with traditional fairy tales but less familiarity with the characteristics,
elements, and literary devices in animal tales such as trickster tales, fables, and "why" or *pourquoi*
tales. I viewed this as positive, and I knew I could build on some of the characteristics students
already were aware of in fairy tales as we extended their understanding of folktales. Consequently, I
decided it was important to expose them to additional types of folktales they were less familiar with
so they could gain a better understanding of their common features, typical form, and
organizational structure. Knowing and recognizing how various genres are organized and presented
helps readers anticipate the type of text to be read, which in turn can support comprehension.
Moreover, I was aware that according to the state standards and the district curriculum, students
needed to be able to read, understand, and discuss various types of folktales, such as beast tales of
trickery, fables, legends, and myths. I decided to begin with trickster tales because of their high
interest, humor, and relatively identifiable characteristics.

Focus

Being familiar with what students knew helped me make better decisions about what else I
needed to teach. Additionally, because I was aware of their prior knowledge and experiences
with folktales, I was able to make links between what they already knew and what I was
teaching. Because folktales offer students many opportunities to hear rich language and a wide
variety of language patterns, I began by immersing students in many trickster tales in both read-
alouds and shared reading focus lessons. Trickster tales occur in a variety of cultures, so we
selected various tales that honored the cultures of the students in the class. As we read different
trickster tales, I listed on a chart the characteristics we were noticing from tale to tale. One of the
students' favorite texts was Virginia Hamilton's *A Ring of Tricksters* (1997). This anthology
includes tales from America, the West Indies, and Africa. As students gained background
experience through reading and talking about trickster tales as a whole group, I decided to pull
together small groups for guided reading so students could read, analyze, and talk about the
different aspects and characteristics of the trickster tales. I chose texts that were in line with

Trickster Tales in Folk Literature

Trickster tales work well when read aloud and have a wide appeal across grade levels. Below is a list of characteristics of these kinds of folktales, followed by a list of picture book trickster tales.

Characteristics of Trickster Tales

- Trickster figures exist in nearly every culture. Some trickster figures include the raven, coyote, fox, rabbit, spider, badger, and turtle.

- Often a very human-acting animal uses wit and cunning to take advantage of bigger and stronger animals. Tricksters can assume a human shape at times.

- Tricksters often use wit, pranks, deceit, and mischief to triumph over a more powerful creature/character.

- Tricksters do not always prevail, as they can be foolish or the victim of another's prank.

- Trickster tales are usually brief and direct, with fast-moving plots.

- Often the story relies on one action, a trick or prank, as the solution to the problem.

- The tales usually end in a clever way that surprises and amuses the reader and makes the tale memorable.

- The trickster figure is often the combination of the best and worst of humanity.

- The tales often teach about life, usually with lessons about personal traits and getting along with others.

Selected Trickster Tales

- *The Fortune-Tellers* by Lloyd Alexander (Puffin, 1997)
- *With a Whoop and a Holler* by Nancy Van Laan (Atheneum, 1998)
- *Uncle Remus: The Complete Tales* by Julius Lester (Dial, 1999)
- *Nelson Mandela's Favorite African Folktales* (Norton, 2002)
- *A Ring of Tricksters* by Virginia Hamilton (Blue Sky Press, 1997)
- *The People Could Fly: American Black Folktales* by Virginia Hamilton (Knopf, 2000)
- *How Rabbit Tricked Otter and Other Cherokee Trickster Stories* by Gayle Ross (Parabola, 2003)
- *Iktomi and the Boulder* by Paul Goble (Orchard, 1991) (See also the other Iktomi tales by Paul Goble)
- *The Cow-Tail Switch and Other West African Stories* by Harold Courlander and George Herzog (Owlet, 1987)

students' reading abilities but that would stretch them in terms of reading and understanding the common features of trickster tales including types of characters, settings, actions, typical language, and overall form and structure.

Connect to Previous Lessons

For these six students, I selected a short trickster tale from Africa: "The Red and Blue Coat: A Trickster Tale from the Congo," geared to the ability level of all the readers in the group. In this narrative text, the trickster uses deceit and a few antics to get the better of two close friends. Like many trickster tales, it's brief and has a fast-moving plot. This guided reading lesson builds on the previous discussions about trickster tales in our read-aloud and shared reading lessons.

Before Reading: Tune In to the Text
(approximately 6 minutes)

I began the guided reading lesson by asking the students to think about what they already knew about trickster tales. By thinking and reflecting on the common elements of trickster tales from previous read-alouds and shared reading lessons, students would be able to use that information to predict what they expected to encounter in this particular text. We discussed some of their ideas and how they might relate to the text we would be reading.

Lesson Dialogue	Notes
As you know, we've been reading and talking about trickster tales. We've found out that there are certain things that can tip us off that it's a trickster tale. In other words, when we read a trickster tale, we can usually expect certain elements or features. Today I want you to read a trickster tale on your own. But before we begin reading, I want you to think about what elements or features you'll probably come across as you read the trickster tale. Turn to your elbow partner and discuss what you expect you'll come across.	I remind students of the kinds of text we've been reading and foreshadow what we are about to read. I set the stage for the reading by asking students to bring to mind what they already know about the elements in the trickster tales we discussed during previous read-aloud and shared reading lessons. Requesting students to turn and talk is a familiar technique used in whole-group and small-group settings. Students need opportunities to talk both teacher-to-student and student-to-student. While students talk with a partner, I eavesdrop on the conversations to listen for the various elements they expect to encounter in the texts, so I have an idea what they recall from previous lessons. Paying attention to the partner conversations also helps me link their thoughts and ideas across the guided reading lesson when possible.
Mrs. S.: *Let's share some of what you talked about.*	
Alan: *Well, Megan and I thought there will probably be an animal trickster like Anansi the Spider or Brer Rabbit.*	
Megan: *We thought the trickster would probably play a prank or trick on another character. Kind of like Anansi did to the tiger and alligator in the stories we read.*	I invite students to share what they talked about with their elbow partner to find out the common characteristics in trickster tales they're beginning
Osmin: *And we said that someone would fall for the trick. Most of the time someone does.*	

(continued on next page)

Lesson Dialogue	Notes
Keona: *We thought maybe the trickster will learn a lesson from the trick or prank. Sometimes there's a kind of lesson the characters learn.*	to recognize and come to expect even before reading. Furthermore, it's an opportunity for me to assess what they've learned from previous read-aloud and shared reading lessons. When we value students' talk and thinking, they become more conscious of their thoughts, views, and opinions as meaningful and important. Talking not only invites students to think about their own learning, it contributes to other's understanding and learning.
Saad: *We were wondering if there would be a smaller animal that is the trickster. In some of the stories we read, the littler animal is the one that outsmarts the bigger animal.*	
Mrs. S.: *Okay. Keep those ideas in mind and let's see what we can gather from reading the title, subtitle, and looking at the map in the text before you begin reading. The name of the story is "The Red and Blue Coat: A Trickster Tale from the Congo." What information can you pick up from just the title, subtitle, and the map?*	I remind students to keep the discussion in mind as I read the title of the trickster tale. I ask them to think about what they know from reading the title and subtitle and looking at the visual of the map.
Saad: *Alan's right. It's going to be a trickster tale, which means someone is going to get tricked. It says it right here: "A Trickster Tale from the Congo."* (Saad points to the subtitle.)	Readers draw upon, compare, and integrate their prior experience and information from the text to make predictions and speculations. It's important for students to predict and have ways of confirming predictions along the way.
Keona: *Yeah, someone is going to get tricked, and I think there's going to be a trickster in the story that tries to outwit another character. It's going to have something to do with a red and blue coat. I think that's going to be important because it's in the title.*	The students and I have been talking about following a line of thinking during discussions. Here we see Keona following Saad's initial line of thinking, and later Katie picks up on Keona's line of thinking. It's important for students to learn how to listen to one another and expand on what has been said, when possible.
Katie: *I think that, too. One of the main characters is going to try to annoy one of the other characters. He's going to do something he thinks is intentionally funny. He will pull a prank or joke. Like when I told my brother it was time to get up for school, and he got up and got dressed before he remembered it was Saturday. But in this story, I think it will have something to do with the coats, too.*	
Alan: *The story is from the Congo in Africa. It shows here on the map where that is.*	
Mrs. S.: *Why do you think the author included the map for the reader?*	I ask the students to expand on their thinking and infer why the map would be included in the selection for the reader.
Osmin: *I think it's so the reader knows where this trickster tale came from. Just like some of the trickster tales we read came from other countries.*	Notice that from students' responses I can gather what they understand about trickster tales. As they talk, I jot

(continued on next page)

Lesson Dialogue	Notes
Mrs. S.: *Okay, so far we're saying in trickster tales there will be a character that is the trickster. Also, there will be another character that will be tricked or fooled by the trickster. And you noticed that this particular tale is from Africa. So, folktales come to us from different cultures and places in the world.* *Now it's time to read. In this trickster tale, the trickster decides to test the friendship of two really good friends, or close companions. Read to find how he does this. What exactly does the trickster do? Also, be ready to talk about whether you think the friends were truly good friends. If you get finished early, mark the places in your text that support your thinking with a "P" to show that's where it "proves" whether or not you think they were truly good friends. Remember, you can use your marker to code the text to help yourself think as you read. I want you to pay special attention to any part that you're confused by or unsure of. Be sure to mark that part. We'll talk about it after we all finish reading.*	down their ideas on a large sheet of paper clipped to an easel so we can refer to their ideas after reading. Being familiar with some of the prevailing characteristics of narrative texts helps readers organize their story understanding and recall. Categories such as setting, character, problem, goal, events, action, outcome, resolution, and theme are parts of story structure readers may use as they read and gather meaning from the text. I give students a brief introduction so they have an idea of what the tale will be about. I purposely use the word *companions*, found in the first paragraph of the text in my introduction, because some students may not be familiar with the word. I don't bring them into the text to find the word, because I am counting on students using the context clues to infer the meaning. Their understanding of the meaning of the word is something I can determine after reading. I set a purpose for reading. Students who finish early have a follow-up task. I remind students to think as they read, to code the text if it will help them, and to be sure to notice when and where they're confused.

During Reading: Students Read the Text (approximately 5 minutes)

During the reading the students have an option of recording their thinking by marking the text as they read. Marking the text can heighten readers' awareness. It can make it easier for some students to retrieve information for discussion or to use as a reference when locating specific information after reading. Codes and marks can help readers when they return to the text to explain their thinking, locate details, describe surprising or interesting parts, or discuss something that confused them or that they didn't understand. Here are some of the codes the students have learned to use while reading:

+   It's interesting.

*   It surprised me.

L   It's something I've learned. (This is a code more prevalently used in nonfiction texts.)

?   I'm confused; I don't get it. (This may be confusion at the word, sentence, or text level.)

    Students usually write on consumable texts with a fine-line colored marker or highlighter. They mark by circling, underlining, or placing codes next to various sections of text. Students use sticky-notes or bookmarks in texts that are routinely circulated and used by others.

As students read the selection I observed where and how they marked the text. I noticed which places students marked with a question mark, indicating that they didn't understand something or that they might be confused, so I would be sure they brought these questions to the after-reading discussion.

After Reading: Return to the Focus and Dig Deeper (approximately 9 minutes)

When students finished reading the text, we discussed how the trickster tested the friendship of the two friends. Students returned to the text during the discussion to provide the evidence they needed to make their point. Megan talked about how surprised she was that two friends would argue and actually fight over something as silly as the color of a coat. Osmin responded by saying, "Well, sometimes people overreact and don't stop to think about it ahead of time. They just act, and it's later that they realize they did something that wasn't really right or nice." At this point, Alan brought the group back to the text by saying, "In the last paragraph the trickster explains it to the friends." Alan read the text:

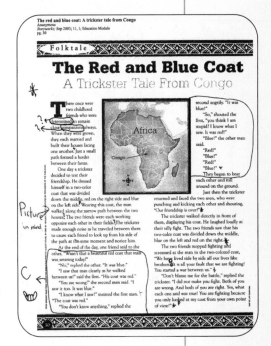

"Don't blame me for the battle," replied the trickster. "I did not make you fight. Both of you are wrong. And both of you are right. Yes, what each one said was true! You are fighting because you only looked at my coat from your own point of view!"

Alan continued, "He means that they each saw it their way—as they wanted to see it. You have to try to understand why somebody says or does something, not just think of how you would say or do something." Keona added, "Sometimes people fight over little things and it turns into something big." The students began talking about the idea of true friends and what friendship means.

Next, Megan brought up what confused her and explained how she'd sorted it out while reading. "At first I was confused about the coat and how it had different colors—right here. [She points to paragraph two.] I didn't get it at first. But then I went back and reread it, and then I understood. I also wasn't sure what *companion* meant. I put a question mark next to it. I kept reading, and it was in the next to last paragraph where I figured it out." She began to read the next to last paragraph:

The two friends stopped fighting and screamed at the man in the two-colored coat, "We have lived side by side all our lives like brothers! It is all your fault that we are fighting! You started a war between us!

"After that," Megan continued, "I went back to reread the sentence with the word *companion* in it again, and I realized it was like best friends or almost like brothers."

The group talked about how readers can reread when they're confused, or continue reading on to see if context will help clarify the meaning; Megan had successfully employed both these strategies. When students discuss the thinking and problem solving they do as they read, it makes their reading process visible for other students and their teacher.

We returned to the chart we'd started at the beginning of the lesson, which listed what we'd expected to find in the text. Together, we clarified our initial ideas and added to the list of trickster-tale characteristics. The students examined some of the similarities and differences between Anansi the Spider and Brer Rabbit—two tricksters they'd met in previous read-alouds— and the trickster in today's guided reading selection. They noticed that all the previous tales we'd read had talking animals rather than people, that some tales ended with the trickster prevailing and others with the trickster being outwitted, and that in each tale there was a lesson to be learned, either by the trickster or by those who fell prey to him. Katie summarized her deeper understanding of trickster tales during the discussion with this remark, "I think I get it. Folktales were stories told and passed down over the years so people could learn more about each other and life. The animals kind of represent people and how they act. Every time we read another folktale, it helps us learn that people are different and that they sometimes act in different ways." Katie shared her insightful remark with the rest of the class that day during the share time of reading workshop. Additionally, students referred to her comment about folktales at various times as our genre study of trickster tales continued and later expanded into reading and discussing fables.

Observations About the Lesson and Lesson Follow-Up

Immersing students in a genre study helps them understand the unique features of the genre, both in terms of text structure and in terms of authority, perspective, and language. As you introduce a genre to students, read aloud representative texts and provide multiple opportunities for students to read them during shared, guided, and independent reading times. Develop lists of characteristics of the genre with your students to help them recognize and become familiar with it. And use think-alouds to model how you pay attention to these features in order to help you read and understand the text.

TIPS AND TECHNIQUES

Reading Widely

Remember, it's important to help students learn how to read and understand many genres. During individual reading conferences, examine students' reading logs to determine the kinds of texts they are choosing for themselves during independent reading. If students are reading too narrowly, help them set goals to read more widely and experience a variety of genres.

Guided Reading Lesson 4:
Understanding Perspective
and Point of View Through Inferring
from a Piece of Historical Fiction

Materials

"Sacajawea: A Teen Who Led the Way" (page 160), whiteboard easel or chart paper, markers

What I Noticed

During individual reading conferences with Terry Scott's sixth-grade class, I noticed that some students, while reading their self-selected texts, had difficulty identifying the point of view the story was being told from. They could identify various characters yet were unclear who was telling the story. I also noticed as I conferred and discussed the text events with students that others, although they recognized who was narrating the story, had difficulty going beyond the exact words of the text to make inferences and draw conclusions about the characters based on their actions and the events.

Additionally, when Terry and I analyzed the results of the *Developmental Reading Assessment* (DRA), we noticed that well over half of the students had difficulty inferring from the texts they read during the assessment, another sign that this was an area of need.

Focus

To help students begin to understand perspective and point of view and to interpret and make inferences, Terry and I planned a series of mini-lessons for the whole class before moving directly into small group guided reading lessons. We like to use books by Chris Van Allsburg to teach students more about a character's perspective. His picture books are filled with clues that the reader must put together in order to fully understand the actions and thoughts of the characters in the text.

We started by reading *The Wretched Stone* aloud to students. As we read, we stopped to discuss who was telling the story and what we could infer from the characters' actions, thoughts, and words. We asked students to cite evidence from the text that backed up their thinking. Over the course of a few days our workshop focus lessons moved from read-aloud to shared reading of lifted text. We made overhead transparencies of a few selected pages of the text from the book. That way, as we revisited the text, all students could see, read, and easily refer to the page of text to support their thinking and reasoning.

It was slow going at first because students only could provide limited evidence to back up their thinking. Some of the students weren't used to taking the time to return to a text to substantiate their way of thinking and reasoning. When asked to explain why they thought in a particular way, at first it wasn't uncommon to hear "Just because I think that" or "I don't know, I just do." So we gave students a chance to watch us demonstrate our thinking and how we used words from the text to substantiate our own reasoning. Students began to pick up on ways of validating their thinking and finding evidence in the text. Some of the questions and statements that helped them move into providing evidence included the following:

- *What in the text makes you think that?*
- *Can you explain why you think that?*
- *Would you please support your thinking?*
- *I think the character (feels, thinks, wants)_____ because_____.*
- *I made that inference because I read [because I thought]_____.*
- *I think that happened in the story because_____.*

These whole-group mini-lessons helped lay the groundwork so we could now move the same focus for instruction into small-group guided reading lessons. Terry and I selected guided reading texts that would help students continue to gain a better understanding of the perspectives portrayed by the characters and involved making inferences based on the events of the story and the actions, thoughts, and words of the characters. We chose texts that had varying perspectives and points of view and that required readers to draw inferences about the characters. Additionally, we selected different text types—historical fiction, realistic fiction, folktales, and fantasy. Readers need repeated experiences with a strategy in many different types of text.

Connect to Previous Lessons

For the six students in my guided reading group, I selected a historical fiction excerpt, "Sacajawea: A Teen Who Led the Way," by Joseph Bruchac. In this fictionalized excerpt, Sacajawea's voice

Tips and Techniques

When first beginning to teach readers how to make inferences, plan both read-aloud and shared reading focus lessons to help them learn and practice how to go beyond the literal meaning of the text and read between the lines. Select a variety of texts to read to and with the students, including cartoons, riddles, poetry, realistic and historical fiction picture books, and content-related texts. Demonstrate using a think-aloud to show students how you use your background knowledge and the clues from the text to figure out and understand more from the reading when authors don't tell everything about the story in the words themselves. With your support and guidance, give students a chance to make inferences as they read texts during shared and guided reading. Encourage them to repeatedly return to the text for evidence from both the words and illustrations to support their reasoning and assumptions. Watch for times readers make inferences about characters' intentions, characteristics, and events as they read their self-selected texts. Keep anecdotal records of your observations and don't forget to have readers share their learning and justify their thinking, especially during the reading workshop share time.

Perspective and Point of View

Stories are often told from a particular perspective and point of view. The perspective refers to *who* tells us the story—the character chosen to tell the story. Point of view refers to *how* the story is told—the source and scope of the narrative point. Sometimes, it is described as the position or point of view the narrator takes when telling the story. The various positions or points of view writers may draw upon usually fall into the following categories.

- **First person** (pronoun *I*)—The narrator is a character in the story. The story is told in her voice. The action is seen through that character's eyes.

- **Second person** (pronoun *you*)—The narrator is supposedly the reader. The story is told as if it is happening to the reader. This point of view is the least used, because it is often awkward and difficult to make work well. It is occasionally used in young adult fiction such as the Choose Your Own Adventure book series.

- **Third person, limited** (pronouns *he, she, it*)—The narrator knows the thoughts, feelings, and memories of (usually) the main character, or protagonist, but no other characters. The way people, places, and events appear to that character is the way they appear to the reader. It may help to think of the third-person narrator as a camera gazing over the shoulder of the main character recording what happens for the reader. This point of view is probably the most used in mainstream fiction.

- **Third person, omniscient** (pronouns *he, she, they*)—The story is told by an all-knowing narrator who can describe to the reader the thoughts, actions, and feelings of all characters. Being omniscient, the narrator is privy to all things past and present and witnesses all events, even some that no characters witness. The omniscient narrator permits the reader to consider the characters' multiple perspectives. This point of view offers the reader a bird's-eye view of the story.

Most texts for younger students are told in the first person or third person, limited.

The point of view from which a story is told inevitably affects our understanding of the character's actions by filtering what is told through his or her own perspective. The perspective of a story often reveals a character's thoughts, feelings, and actions within a particular time and place. Reading texts that offer a variety of perspectives helps students question, examine, and interpret their own viewpoints, experiences, and perceptions. Texts that offer varying perspectives help students relate to others and imagine what it is like to walk in someone else's shoes. Moreover, reading texts with varying perspectives provides opportunities for students to critically consider if there are other perspectives that might not be included or are left out entirely. As students read more demanding fictional texts, it is important that they not only know what they think about what they're reading, but also that they understand the various perspectives of others (Fountas and Pinnell, 2000).

recounts the beginning of the journey she embarks on with Lewis and Clark to her now-grown son. This particular text dovetailed nicely with what the students had been studying in social studies about the opening of the West with the Lewis and Clark expedition. In their course of study, students had built a fair amount of background knowledge about the expedition and related historical events during that period.

Before Reading: Tune In to the Text (approximately 6 minutes)

I began the guided reading lesson by asking students to reflect on previous lessons and conversations we had about why it was important for the reader to know who's narrating the story. Having an understanding of whose perspective a story is told from helps readers gain insight and understanding from the point of view they move through in the story. As part of the before-reading time, I read aloud the introduction to the passage as students followed along. We discussed and listed on a chart the information students learned from the text and already knew about the Sacajawea and the Lewis and Clark expedition so we could refer and add to it later. The reading of this text was divided into two parts. After reading, the students discussed the problems those on expedition faced, according to Sacajawea, and how her perspective differed from those of Lewis and Clark.

Lesson Dialogue	Notes
Mrs. S.: *In our read-aloud and shared reading time, we've been talking about how important it is to pay attention to who's narrating or telling a story when we're reading. Why should we keep in mind who's telling the story?*	I link previous lessons and texts we've been reading in both read-aloud and shared reading to today's reading. I ask students to reflect on and briefly discuss what they've learned about point of view and the position the narrator takes in a text. Carrying previous learning from read-aloud and shared reading into guided reading helps students reevaluate their thinking. Students begin to see that what they've learned can be used in many different kinds of texts and learning situations.
Gabby: *It helps us know who the main character is and what they're thinking and doing.*	
Elijah: *When you know who's telling the story you know whose point of view it is, and that can help you understand the story and sometimes that person better. Like in a story I was reading about Jackie Robinson. It was like a narrator telling me about his life. It's like he's sitting there telling me what he knows about Jackie Robinson. I think that's told in the third person because it says* he *or his name pretty much all the way through.*	
Mrs. S.: *Gabby and Elijah, those are helpful points. In today's reading, it will be important for you to pay attention to who is telling the story and to keep that in mind as*	I acknowledge the students' thinking and ideas. I state the importance of knowing and keeping in mind from whose point of view the text is told. I introduce the title and the author.

(continued on next page)

Lesson Dialogue	Notes
you read it. The name of the story you're going to read is "Sacajawea: A Teen Who Led the Way." It is an excerpt from a novel called Sacajawea *by Joseph Bruchac. Do you know what an excerpt is?*	I explain that the passage is an excerpt from a novel. I raise a question about the meaning of an excerpt to probe students' understanding.
Jaden: *It means that it's not the whole story. It's a piece or part of it.*	
Mrs. S.: *Exactly. This text you're going to read today is a small piece from Bruchac's novel. If you flip to the second page you'll see a picture of his novel. (Students look quickly and then return to the first page.) Now, take a moment to look at the picture and read the caption at the top of the page. Do you have any idea what kind of text this is?*	I validate Jaden's explanation. I prompt students to look at the picture and read the caption to call attention to the genre of the text.
Senga: *Historical fiction. I can tell from the picture of Sacajawea and Lewis and Clark and the title, too.*	
Mrs. S.: *Yes, in this historical fiction excerpt, Sacajawea tells about the Lewis and Clark journey from her point of view. It's told in the first person—which means she tells us the story through her voice and eyes. The introduction—the section that is written in italics—is important because it gives the reader some background about the excerpt. Listen and follow along while I read the portion here in italics. (I point to the section in italics and then begin to read.)*	Here I explain whose point of view the excerpt will be told from. Knowing ahead of time that Sacajawea is describing her perspective on the journey in the passage and that the story is told from her point of view supports the readers from the start. Notice that I've decided to read the introduction in italics to the students as they follow along. I do this because of the unusual font and so I can keep the lesson moving and get them into the reading of the passage. As I read the introduction, I briefly point out the pronunciation key for Sacajawea and mention how we can tell from the use of the capital letters which syllables are accented, or said more strongly.
Mrs. S.: *So what have we learned from the text by reading just this little bit? (I begin to jot down points students make.)*	I prompt students to elaborate on what they've learned from this section of text. As they share, I jot down their responses and ideas on a chart so we can refer to them later in our discussions. I prompt Annie for further thinking and clarification.
Annie: *It says here that an older Sacajawea is telling it to her son.*	
Mrs. S.: *Yes. And why is that important for us to know?*	
Annie: *Because she's thinking back on what happened.*	
Mrs. S.: *It's a flashback, isn't it? And if she's thinking back on it, then what can we infer about her son?*	I feed in the literary device the author has used in this text. I prompt students to make an inference about Sacajawea's son based on what we know and the clues from the text of when she is telling us the story.
Herman: *He's older, too. Maybe he's an adult by now and she's telling him about the expedition.*	

(continued on next page)

Lesson Dialogue	Notes
Mrs. S.: *When we read on, let's see if there's more information that supports that. What else have we learned?*	Here I call for students to be on the lookout for places in the text as they read that provide us with additional confirmation that Sacajawea's son is older or an adult.
Gabby: *She was only 16 years old when she started the journey with Lewis and Clark. And her baby Pomp traveled with her.*	Students continue to expand upon and gather additional information about the genre, title, and this significant event from the introduction.
Mrs. S.: *Ah, Gabby, you have a good memory from our other readings, you recall Sacajawea's son's name.*	
Jaden: *It says they went from the Mississippi River to the Pacific Ocean and the expedition lasted three years.*	
Senga: *Sacajawea's name means "Bird Woman" in her language. And she was from the Shoshone tribe.*	
Mrs. S.: *I jotted your ideas down—look at all we've gathered so far. We've just read a small amount and have come up with quite a bit of information. Readers, it's important to read an introduction like this when a book or text provides it and not to just skip over it. Do you see just how much important information this little section in italics provided us?*	I remind students how important it is to read introductions and I stress just how much information they can provide the reader. I've recently noticed during individual reading conferences that some students have been skipping over text features such as the introduction, preface, and/or headings in their self-selected independent texts. Reading and talking about the information the introduction provided us in this text is a way I can give emphasis to and help students see the important information various text features, such as an introduction, provide the reader.
Readers, I know you've been talking about the Lewis and Clark expedition in social studies. Is there anything else you know or expect might be included in the text that you want to add to the chart before you begin reading? (I add a few more details to the chart that students share.)	I ask students to draw on additional background knowledge and relate any further information they may know before reading.
It will help you when you read today to keep in mind what you've been learning and already know about the Lewis and Clark expedition.	I remind students to think about what they know as they read. When students are aware of what they know about a topic, they are more likely to recognize when they've learned something new or important when reading.
We're going to break our reading of this text into two parts. We'll stop and talk about what you've read after each part. Part 1 includes the first seven paragraphs. Mark that now so you'll know where to stop. Paragraph seven ends with "the mice gather them in great numbers." (I wait while students mark the point to stop.) When everyone has read to the end of the first part, we'll stop and discuss what we've read. Then we'll read the last part, which	Here I explain how the reading will go in today's lesson. I have students find and mark the first stopping point in their reading. I remind students from whose point of view the story is told. I draw attention to and give an example of the unusual language in the story. I set a purpose for reading and give early finishers a task. I reveal what they will need to

(continued on next page)

Lesson Dialogue	Notes
will take us to the end of the text. Remember, this story is told from Sacajawea's point of view-through her eyes. You'll notice that some of the language in the text is very different from the way we speak today. Listen to this example, "They talked especially about the One Who Walks Like a Man." *As you read the first part, pay attention to what concerned Sacajawea. What were some of the problems she and the others faced on the journey? Also, look for ways in which they resolved some of the problems along the way. It's not always clear, so you'll have to draw some inferences from her words. You can use your marker to code the text to help keep track of your thinking as you read. If you finish early, go back to make sure you can provide evidence in the text of her concerns, problems, and solutions. (I jot down the purpose for reading on a white board.) Okay, begin reading the first part and be ready to talk about what you find out.*	do as a reader—draw some inferences—so they can anticipate they will need to do some work reading between the lines. I remind students that they can write on the text to keep track of their thinking. I jot down the purpose for reading on a whiteboard to remind students of their reason for reading this first part and what to do if they finish reading early.

During Reading: Read the text (approximately 4 minutes)

As the students silently read the first part of the selection about Sacajawea, I asked Senga to read aloud the first two paragraphs of the text. As she read, I took brief anecdotal notes of what I observed so I could talk to her about what I noticed about her reading. The anecdotal notes show that far more was revealed about Senga's thinking and processing as a reader in what was about a two-minute exchange than merely her understanding of Sacajawea's perspective within the context of this lesson.

2/15 Senga   GR text "Sacajawea"

Read first two paragraphs aloud
- monitors reading & understanding
- pauses; rereads; problem-solves "provisions" pro/vi/sions; breaks into parts; repeated word; read on; fast word work on run

Brief discussion
- explains meaning of "provisions" and use of context to get it
- explains initial confusion with phrase "One who walks like a man"; goes into text and shows how she used the sentence that follows it to figure out meaning.

Anecdotal notes taken on Senga's reading

After Reading the First Part: Return to the Focus and Dig Deeper to Extend Thinking About the Text (approximately 5 minutes)

When the students finished reading the first part, we stopped to briefly discuss the reading. Students returned to the text during the discussion to provide the evidence they needed to make their various points or search for more information. Our after-reading discussion follows.

Lesson Dialogue	Notes
Mrs. S.: *I noticed a number of you made notes in the margins as you read. That's a good way to keep track of your thinking while you're reading. Let's begin by discussing what you found out about Sacajawea's concerns. What were some of her concerns on the journey?*	It's important to acknowledge and encourage students to monitor their thinking as they read. By making notes and visual representations or sketches in the margins, students stay on top of meaning and build understanding as they read. Although I don't directly ask students what they've written in the margins at this point, our discussion often bring their ideas, interpretations, sources of confusion, and misconceptions to light. Here I begin the discussion by coming back to the purpose for reading the first part of the text.
Elijah: *Well, they needed to hunt to survive. They brought food along, like dried salted meat, but it wouldn't be enough to last them on the whole trip.*	
Jaden: *Yeah, because there were 20 people. I thought it was just Lewis, Clark, and Sacajawea. I didn't realize so many people went along. Now I can see why food would be a problem. They had to feed a lot of people.*	Notice how Elijah, Jaden, and Herman follow a line of thinking as they discuss one of the concerns.
Herman: *I think that's why they called it an expedition because there were lots of people.*	
Annie: *I have a question mark at "provisions." I wasn't sure what it meant until I read on. Then it said, "including salted meat and food that had been dried," and that's when I realized it means food or supplies.*	Here Herman refers to a word he wasn't sure about and explains for the other students how he figured out the meaning of it. When students share the strategies they know how to use, in order to figure out new words and the meaning, it provides a model for how other readers might employ similar strategies.
Mrs. S.: *Good reading work, Annie. You read on to see if you could gather more information you could use to figure out, or infer, the meaning of that word. Senga did that with the word* provisions *too, when I was reading with her. What other concerns did Sacajawea have that you read about?*	I deliberately restate what Annie has done to infer the meaning of *provisions* and validate the way in which Senga did something similar. Both students know strategies for approaching difficult words. I bring the group back to our purpose for reading by restating the question on the whiteboard.
Gabby: *It said the two captains were good hunters so she knew they could hunt for food. But she was worried about them hunting for grizzly bears. I think she thought a bear might kill them or maybe hurt them.*	
Mrs. S.: *Which words made you think that?*	I prompt Gabby to support her inference with evidence from the text.
Gabby: *The part where it says, "If you do not show respect to the bear, he will not respect you. . . . I worried when I heard the captains talk with excitement about hunting the grizzly bear. I hoped they would remember to respect him."*	Here Gabby returns to the text and reads the part she noticed in the text. It's important for students to go back into the text to substantiate their thinking.

(continued on next page)

Lesson Dialogue	Notes
Senga: *At first I didn't know what she meant by "the One Who Walks Like a Man," and then I read on and realized it was a bear. She meant it was walking on its hind legs like a man. I think Gabby is right—she's worried they might get hurt.*	Senga explains a part that was confusing and how she was able to infer the meaning as she picked up on more of the clues from the text. She also validates Gabby's earlier inference by agreeing with it.
Jaden: *Yeah, that would slow the expedition down or maybe even end it if they died.*	Jaden adds his own inference when he states what it would mean to the expedition if something happened to Lewis or Clark.
Elijah: *She was also worried they'd run out of animals when they got way up into the mountains.*	Elijah brings the discussion back to another of Sacajawea's possible concerns.
Annie: *She knew how to find roots in the earth that the harvester mice put there in a storage place in the ground.*	Annie explains how Sacajawea was able to solve that problem.
Mrs. S.: *Take us to that part and read it.*	Here I prompt Annie to support her thinking with proof from the text.
(Annie reads the part about finding the great pile of driftwood on the riverbank and breaking through to the mound of white roots the mice gathered.)	
Mrs. S.: *What does it mean when Sacajawea asks, "Where were you then? Do you not remember? You were right there in your cradleboard."*	I draw students' attention to a part in the text where there is a series of questions. I ask them to clarify what they mean and why the author has included them.
Herman: *It wasn't her asking the questions. It was her son.*	
Gabby: *I think it's her thinking inside her head asking all those questions. If her son said it, he'd have to be talking to himself. He wouldn't be saying, "Do you not remember?" to himself.*	
Mrs. S.: *So, are you saying the "you" in each of those questions refers to her son?*	I clarify Gabby's response and provide more information about who the pronoun *you* refers to in the questions.
Gabby: *Yes.*	
Senga: *It says, "You were right there with me in your cradleboard." I think that means Sacajawea's baby was next to her when she was looking for the roots and she was just thinking those questions.*	
Mrs. S.: *Yes, good thinking. Readers, keep in mind what we read at the beginning in italics. Look back there. (I point to the part and read.) It says here, "Joseph Bruchac imagines an older Sacajawea telling the story to her son." This whole piece is from*	I center the readers' attention on the introduction to clarify confusions about who is telling the story. I reread the text to highlight and confirm that Sacajawea is telling the story to her son.
	(continued on next page)

Lesson Dialogue	Notes
Sacajawea's perspective and her first-person point of view.	
Elijah: *Because it says "I."*	
Mrs. S.: *Yes. It uses the pronoun I. That's a strong clue for the reader it's told in the first person, isn't it?*	I clarify Elijah's response and draw students' attention to how the pronoun *I* is a strong indication for the reader that the story is told in the first person.
Okay, let's read the last part now. In this part, read to find out what other information you can learn from Sacajawea's perspective of the journey with Lewis and Clark. Again, it's not always clear, so you'll have to put together the clues that the author gives and what you already know to draw some inferences from her words. You can use your marker to code the text to help keep track of your thinking as you read. If you finish early, go back to make sure you can provide evidence in the text of what else you've learned. If it would help to refresh your memory, feel free to take time to read the last paragraph in the first part we read before reading the next part. Okay, begin reading. (I jot down the purpose for reading the second part on the whiteboard.)	Here I am setting the purpose for reading the last part of the text. I remind the students that they will once again need to read between the lines by putting the author's clues together with what they already know. I let them know that they can keep track of their thinking as they read and what to do if they finish early. I intentionally suggest the idea of rereading a small portion of the previously read text to help students gather some of the meaning before reading on. I jot down the purpose for reading on the whiteboard to remind students of the reason for reading this next part.

After Reading the Second Part: Return to the Focus and Dig Deeper to Extend Thinking About the Text (approximately 6 minutes)

When the students finished reading the second part of the text, I started by asking them, "What did you think of this short piece about Sacajawea?" The students engaged in a lively discussion, often reading from the text to support their assertions. The discussion ended with students speculating about how different Lewis and Clark's perspective of the journey would be from Sacajawea's.

Since students' interest about other perspectives of the expedition was piqued during the discussion, I thought some of them might like to choose the entire *Sacajawea* novel by Joseph Bruchac to read independently. I borrowed the book from the school library the following day. I met briefly with the same group of students again to give a book talk about the novel, explaining that Sacajawea and William Clark tell, in alternating points of view, about the danger, hardship, and excitement along their journey. I thought because the book provided two points of view—each told in the first person—that some of the students' questions about how Sacajawea's and Clark's perspectives about the journey differed might be answered. During the book talk, I showed students how each Sacajawea chapter began with a traditional Shoshone folktale and the Clark chapters included excerpts from Clark's and Lewis's journals. Gabby responded with great interest and the next day during the independent reading time of reading workshop, she settled in to begin the book.

Final Thoughts

To understand others' perspectives, students need to make inferences from the actions, feelings, and experiences of those they read about in the text, while at the same time tap into their own background knowledge and experiences. Students must also be able to ask questions and to look for answers from specific information in the text as well as to make inferences from implied meanings in the text in order to grasp the important ideas. As we teach for strategic actions in our guided reading lessons, it's important to note how well students are using and applying them as they read. Look for evidence of when and how students use their strategy knowledge as they meet more demanding texts and different genres.

In Closing

Throughout this book I've tried to emphasize that, in order to meet the diverse needs of students in any intermediate class, you need to use a variety of approaches in the teaching of reading in a comprehensive literacy framework. You should provide a range of experiences with read-alouds, shared reading, guided reading, and independent reading. Each approach offers a different level of support to the reader. In this book, I've highlighted guided reading, in which a teacher and a small group of students have an opportunity to talk, read, and think their way purposefully through a text. The goal of guided reading is to support intermediate students in becoming more accomplished readers. As teachers, we want to develop students who are confident, competent, and discriminating readers who actively think, practice, and employ reading strategies as they read for understanding. We want to grow readers for the real world who choose to read and who show and feel enthusiasm for reading. Our job is really bigger than just teaching students how to read; it's also about them wanting to read so they become lifelong readers.

I hope *Guided Reading in Grades 3–6* offers you some practical and useful ideas to implement guided reading with your intermediate students. May you find joy and success growing the readers you work with each day.

Table of Contents
for Short Guided Reading Passages

Every effort has been made to obtain permission to use the articles reprinted here. We will correct any errors in reprint.

Accidental Delights

Some of the most beloved foods in America were created by regular people—and by accident.

Hanson Gregory licked his lips, eager for his mother to finish preparing his snack. She stood at the stove of their home in Maine, frying a batch of pastries. They were Hanson's favorite food. The flattened cakes cooked in hot oil until they were golden brown. But there was a problem: The centers of the cakes never cooked through. Hanson and everyone else who loved them had to cut out the soggy middle.

On this day in 1847, however, Hanson had an idea. Just as his mother put another cake in the pan, Hanson grabbed a fork and poked a hole in the center. The edges browned, and the entire pastry was cooked. Hanson Gregory, age 15, had just invented the doughnut.

Many of today's most popular products were accidental inventions, according to Stephen Paul Gnass, founder of a Web site dedicated to inventions called InventionConvention.com. "You can put a tremendous amount of time, energy, and effort into developing a specific invention," says Gnass. "Then, BAM!—without any effort on your part, a totally unrelated idea finds you!"

Hanson Gregory isn't the only person to have made a delicious discovery by accident. Potato chips were invented by an angry chef. He decided to play a trick on a customer who kept complaining that his fried potatoes were too thick. A famous sandwich spread—peanut butter—was made because a man couldn't eat meat. His doctor ground up roasted peanuts and mixed them with peanut oil to make a protein-rich food that could be digested easily.

Hanson Gregory never made any money from his discovery, and the doughnut isn't even named for him. But one young inventor did sell his accidental creations. In the winter of 1905, 11-year-old Frank Epperson was stirring soda pop powder and water in a cup on his back porch. He accidentally left the stick in the mixture overnight. The next morning, Frank discovered his drink had frozen with the stick still in the middle. He pulled the stick and frozen mix out of the cup, took a lick, and became the first person ever to eat a Popsicle.

The next summer, Frank made Popsicles in the icebox. At first, he called the frozen treats "Epsicles" (short for "Epperson Icicle") and sold them for five cents each. In 1923, he changed the name to "Popsicle," and the food became an international hit.

Inspired to create your own tasty treat? Your best ideas just might happen by accident.

The Puppy-Raisers

Kids help train puppies for an important mission: to become guide dogs for the blind.

Twelve-year-old Leah adores her golden retriever puppy, Mandy. But in just a few months, Leah knows she will have to give Mandy away forever.

That's because Mandy isn't an ordinary pet, and Leah isn't an ordinary dog owner. Mandy is being trained for an important mission: to become a guide dog for the blind. Leah is a "puppy raiser," charged with providing Mandy with a loving home until the dog is old enough to begin her serious training.

Guide dogs are usually Labrador retrievers, golden retrievers, or German shepherds, all breeds known for their intelligence and reliability. They are bred and trained by special schools across the country to help blind people in their daily activities. By the time training is complete, the dogs should be able to take their owners almost anywhere, from malls to subways to the busiest street intersections.

But this specialized training can't begin until the dogs are about 15 months old, so someone must take care of them until then. That's how kids like Leah can help. "Kids are the perfect choice," says Christine Dickson, manager of puppy placement at The Seeing Eye, a guide dog school in New Jersey. "They have the time and energy to take care of the dogs and teach them basic skills they'll need for training."

Puppy-trainers at The Seeing Eye must be at least 9 years old. Their most important task is to get the dogs used to being in public. "We have to teach them commands like 'rest' and 'forward,'" Leah says. "That's what a blind person will be saying to them." Otherwise, Leah just gives Mandy a lot of love and attention.

Giving up a beloved pet is difficult, but puppy-raisers like Leah understand that their dog will transform the lives of blind people. Just ask Mike Townsend, who has been blind since birth. He never leaves home without his guide dog, Glory. "She's like a pair of glasses with four legs and a tail," he says.

One day several years ago, Mike was waiting in front of an elevator on the eighth floor of an office building. When the elevator doors slid open, Glory wouldn't budge. Mike was frustrated, but he knew to trust his canine companion. Then Mike heard the gasp of someone who could see the elevator. There was no elevator car, just an empty hole leading straight to the basement. Mike refuses to think about what would have happened if he had stepped in. Thanks to Glory—and her trainers—Mike doesn't have to.

Lunch or Junk?

Health Experts Get Tough on School Lunches

It's lunch time at Hall Memorial School, in Connecticut, and 10-year-old Haley Neel is making her way through the food line. Many of her friends are thrilled with the day's lunch selections: pizza and french fries and hot dogs. But Haley feels discouraged. "I use four or five napkins just trying to get the grease off the pizza," she says. "Where are the healthy options?"

Health experts are asking the same question. They say foods high in fat, salt, and sugar should be banned from school lunch programs. This includes some items you might not suspect, like fruit punch, which is loaded with sugar, and macaroni and cheese, which is sky-high in fat and salt. "Children are already consuming too much junk food," says Jen Keller, a dietician at the Physician's Committee for Responsible Medicine. "It's important to offer them only healthy items in school."

It's not that health experts want to deprive kids of foods they like best. They just want to help kids avoid many of the health problems that come with eating large quantities of unhealthful food. Today, 15% of children ages 6 to 11 are obese, or seriously overweight. That's up from just 6.5% in the late 1970s. Poor diet and obesity can cause diseases like type 2 diabetes, which can lead to blindness and kidney problems. As of a few years ago, this disease was so rare in children that it was called "adult onset diabetes." "Many foods that are offered in cafeterias are linked to these problems," Keller says.

Most schools do offer some healthful foods, but experts say that doesn't solve the problem. "Given a choice, most kids are going to choose junk over something healthy," says Pat Thorton, a psychologist who studies obesity in children.

Thorton and other experts agree that schools and parents need to educate kids about making good food choices, both in and out of school. For example, few kids understand that many popular candies, chips, and sodas come in containers that actually contain two or even three servings. And kids need to become skeptical about food advertisements they see on TV and in magazines. "Just because Beyonce sells Pepsi doesn't mean it's a good product for your body," Thorton says.

Of course some kids already seem to know all of this. "The junk food is tempting," says 10-year-old Tim Herbert. "But my parents tell me that if I eat healthy now, I'll have strong bones when I get older."

Inventing a Game

How Basketball Was Born

It was the cold winter of 1891, and the adult students at the Springfield YMCA training school in Massachusetts were growing restless. They hated the boring routine of jumping jacks and weight lifting. Not even the teachers thought these activities were fun, but they had run out of ideas. Finally, the school's director called a meeting. "We need a new indoor game," he told the gathering of exhausted instructors. Then he looked at a young teacher named James Naismith. "You," he said with a pointed finger. "Come up with something. You've got two weeks."

For the next 13 days, Naismith experimented with ideas for a brand-new game. Nothing worked. Kicked balls shattered gym windows. Tackles left students' bodies bruised and bloody after they crashed to the hard wooden floor. But Naismith wouldn't give up. He had one last, desperate idea.

The next morning he rushed to the gym. He grabbed a soccer ball from the equipment room and, as his mystified students watched, hammered two peach baskets to the walls. He then scribbled 13 rules for playing his new game, which he tacked on the gym's bulletin board: Players could not run with the ball. There would be no kicking or tackling. To score a point, a player must toss the ball into the basket.

The new game didn't have a name yet, but it soon would: Basketball.

The first game, on December 21, didn't start smoothly. The players ran with the ball and knocked each other down. Nobody wanted to pass. But the thrill of making a basket soon had the men hooked. They loved the new game, and other classes loved to stop and watch. The game spread to other classes. Even the students at a nearby women's school started to play.

Basketball quickly became a sensation. Students took the game home to their local YMCAs. Colleges like Yale and the University of Iowa began playing regular games. By 1936, the sport became an Olympic event. Ten years later, professional basketball began, and the National Basketball Association soon followed. Sports in America—and the world— would never be the same.

The first game in 1891 didn't have backboards, three-point shots, dribbling, or 7-foot players who earn millions of dollars. But, amazingly, most of Naismith's original rules still hold. So the next time you see a basketball game on TV, remember that it all started one morning, more than a hundred years ago.

> The first game, on December 21, didn't start smoothly. The players ran with the ball and knocked each other down. Nobody wanted to pass. But the thrill of making a basket soon had the men hooked.

Oceans in Danger

Marine Wildlife Is Disappearing

Earlier this year, a group of scientists finished a 10-year project to count tuna, cod, swordfish, and other large fish in the world's oceans. They made a shocking discovery: these fish are almost gone.

Because of too much fishing, almost 90% of the worldwide population of large fish—the ones we usually eat—have disappeared. If we don't act, these animals will totally vanish, and that will affect every animal in the ocean.

No stretch of the ocean is untouched. New fishing technologies like sonar, which uses sound waves to detect fish in deep waters, help fishermen find fish all over the globe. Their huge boats, sometimes up to 100 feet long, can travel for days without refueling, withstand giant waves, and capture 100 tons of flounder or shrimp in a single harvest of their nets.

"There isn't anywhere they can't get to," says Lance Morgan, Chief Scientist at the Marine Conservation Biology Institute. "Everywhere you look, there are too many fishermen."

Demand for fish is growing. Almost a billion people around the world get their protein mostly from fish. Doctors praise seafood for being low in fat. But what seems like a healthful choice for humans is causing a disaster in our oceans. "People are consuming too much," says Morgan.

A single grilled tuna steak costs more than just one animal's life. When fish like tuna disappear from the ecosystem, the ocean's food chain breaks. Animals such as sharks, which normally feast on tuna, starve. Nets can also catch and kill more than their intended targets. The bottom trawl, a huge, weighted net that large ships drag across the ocean floor, traps plenty of shrimp. But, for every pound of shrimp, it also captures 10 pounds of unwanted wildlife. Even worse, the trawl scrapes up the ocean floor, destroying natural habitats. Fish farmers hope to solve these problems by growing fish in captivity. Yet farmers must feed their animals other fish—which means killing more animals from the wild.

While the news may be frightening, recovery is possible. World organizations are urging countries to ban overfishing. Groups here in the United States, like the Environmental Protection Agency, have ordered entire fleets of Pacific cod and halibut fishing boats on the West Coast to stop casting nets that also kill rockfish. The Monterey Bay Aquarium publishes a list of responsible seafood choices for anyone hoping to reap health benefits without contributing to environmental destruction.

"If you care about wildlife, first spend time and think about your own values and ethics," says Morgan. "Then decide what you're going to eat."

For information about good seafood choices, go to: www.mbayaq.org/cr/seafoodwatch.asp.

The Red and Blue Coat

A Trickster Tale From Congo

There once were two childhood friends who were determined to remain close companions always. When they were grown, they each married and built their houses facing one another. Just a small path formed a border between their farms.

One day a trickster decided to test their friendship. He dressed himself in a two-color coat that was divided down the middle, red on the right side and blue on the left side. Wearing this coat, the man walked along the narrow path between the two houses. The two friends were each working opposite each other in their fields. The trickster made enough noise as he traveled between them to cause each friend to look up from his side of the path at the same moment and notice him.

At the end of the day, one friend said to the other, "Wasn't that a beautiful red coat that man was wearing today?"

"No," replied the other. "It was blue."

"I saw that man clearly as he walked between us!" said the first. "His coat was red."

"You are wrong!" the second man said. "I saw it too. It was blue."

"I know what I saw!" insisted the first man. "The coat was red."

"You don't know anything," replied the second angrily. "It was blue!"

"So," shouted the first, "you think I am stupid? I know what I saw. It was red!"

"Blue!" the other man said.

"Red!"

"Blue!"

"Red!"

"Blue!"

They began to beat each other and roll around on the ground.

Just then the trickster returned and faced the two men, who were punching and kicking each other and shouting, "Our friendship is over!"

The trickster walked directly in front of them, displaying his coat. He laughed loudly at their silly fight. The two friends saw that his two-color coat was divided down the middle, blue on the left and red on the right.

The two friends stopped fighting and screamed at the man in the two-colored coat, "We have lived side by side all our lives like brothers! It is all your fault that we are fighting! You started a war between us."

"Don't blame me for the battle," replied the trickster. "I did not make you fight. Both of you are wrong. And both of you are right. Yes, what each one said was true! You are fighting because you only looked at my coat from your own point of view!"

When Wild Animals Become Pets

At the age of six weeks, Lilo seemed like the perfect family pet. His family's 9-year-old girl loved to snuggle with the cat and brush his beautiful striped fur. But as Lilo grew up, he didn't like being brushed. One day, as the little girl approached him, Lilo lashed out at her with a swipe of his massive paw. The girl's arm was injured so badly she needed 50 stitches.

It's rare for a family pet to attack its loving owner. But Lilo should never have been anyone's pet. This cute and playful "cat" was actually a tiger, one of at least 15,000 tigers, lions, leopards, cougars, and other big cats currently kept as pets in American homes and backyard zoos.

Owning a pet tiger or lion, experts say, is a dangerous fad in America. "People love these animals and they love the idea of owning something wild and exotic," says Nicole Paquette of the Animal Protection Institute. "They have no idea how hard it is to care for them."

More than 15,000 tigers and other big cats are kept as pets in the United States. That's more than are living in the wilds of Asia, the tigers' natural habitat.

Tigers like Lilo can grow to weigh 650 pounds. They eat 15 pounds of raw meat per day. Their powerful paws, even when de-clawed, can crush a human skull. Dozens of people each year are injured or killed by pet tigers and other big cats.

The situation can also be deadly for the big cats themselves. Fully-grown cats often end up confined to small cages that are never cleaned because their owners are afraid to get too close. Living in squalid conditions, the cats become sickly and often more aggressive. Many animals die from neglect. Others are sold to rag-tag roadside zoos, or to ranches where hunters are allowed to shoot and kill them for sport.

Shirley Minshew works for the International Fund for Animal Welfare, an organization that rescues abandoned and abused big cats. She helps place some fortunate cats in sanctuaries, private shelters that keep the cats well-fed and safe. But as Minshew says, "most of these sanctuaries are already full." So are big city zoos.

The only solution, experts agree, is for people to stop buying these animals. "Wild animals are exactly that—wild," says Paquette. "Although they can be kept in cages, they are not tamable. They will never be like a dog or a cat. They are wild—and they should be allowed to stay that way."

Standing Up by Sitting Down

The True Story of the Greensboro Sit-in

On February 1, 1960, in the town of Greensboro, North Carolina, four African-American college students sat down on high stools at the lunch counter of the local Woolworth's department store. They weren't sitting down for a cup of coffee or a slice of pie. They were sitting down to change the world, or, at least, a part of it.

Throughout the South, prejudice against African Americans was common. The Woolworth's lunch counter—like many restaurants, hotels, and hospitals—refused to serve African Americans. This cruel and humiliating treatment had many African Americans fed up and saying, "No more!" So, Ezell A. Blair Jr., Franklin McCain, Joseph O'Neil, and David Richmond—the four Greensboro college students—decided to fight back . . . but not with violence. The four men walked into Woolworth's with a clear plan of action. They knew the waitress would refuse to serve them. They knew other customers would treat them rudely. Some were sure to scream and swear and maybe even try to hurt them. But no matter what, the men vowed, they would remain peaceful and polite, even to those who behaved hatefully towards them.

They'd been inspired by civil rights leader Dr. Martin Luther King Jr. (1929–1968). Dr. King urged African Americans to challenge prejudice and demand equal treatment. But he did not believe in using violence to get results. King said that love can lead to understanding, but hate can only lead to more hate. African Americans, he said, must do something extremely difficult: fight violence and hate with peace and love.

The four men in Greensboro believed passionately in the teachings of Dr. King. But as they took their seats at the counter, they had to wonder: would these ideas work?

Indeed they did. By the end of the week, the four were joined by hundreds of other protesters. News of their "sit-in" spread around the country, and soon other groups were protesting at Woolworth's around the country and other segregated restaurants in the South. By July, the lunch counter at Woolworth's was officially open to African Americans. Other restaurants soon followed.

Through their simple act of sitting down, the four men took a bold stand for equality, justice, and peace.

> **Through their simple act of sitting down, the four men took a bold stand for equality, justice, and peace.**

The History of Gum

Fascinating facts about your favorite treat!

Got the urge to chew? Maybe you should go out to the garage and rip off a nice chunk of car tire. Not your idea of a tasty treat? A nice chunk of chewing gum is probably more like it. But there is a link between car tires and chewing gum, as a quick trip through the halls of gum history will show you.

The history of gum begins thousands of years ago, when prehistoric men and women chewed on lumps of tree resin (a sticky brownish substance that oozes from trees). The ancient Greeks chewed on resin, and so did Native Americans. Early settlers to New England loved to chew too. Gum made from spruce tree resin was a popular treat among early Americans.

The first big breakthrough in modern gum technology came in 1869, when a young New Yorker named Thomas Adams began experimenting with chicle (resin from sapodilla trees). He thought he could combine chicle with rubber and invent a new material for making tires.

His experiments were disastrous, but then Adams had another idea. If people couldn't drive on his chicle, maybe they could chew on it! Before long, Adams New York No. 1 chicle gum was all the rage.

By the late 1800s, the gum business was booming. A new product called Dentyne came out, promising to help "dental hygiene."

Around 1900, an inventive gum maker coated small pieces of chicle gum with candy and Chiclets were born. The first bubble gum, called Blibber-Blubber, was invented in 1906, but it never sold. It was so sticky that if it popped on your skin, it was impossible to remove!

It was in 1928 that Walter Diemer accidentally invented Double Bubble, the first successful bubble gum. Diemer was an accountant who liked to experiment with new gum recipes in his spare time. One day, without specifically trying to, he happened to hit upon the perfect bubble gum recipe. He added pink dye because pink was the only color left on the shelf, then carried a five-pound lump of the gum to a local grocery store. It sold out that afternoon.

So, what will "pop" up next in the ever-evolving history of gum? That's something for you to chew on!

> The first bubble gum, called **Blibber-Blubber**, was invented in 1906, but it never sold. It was so sticky that if it popped on your skin, it was **impossible** to remove!

"The History of Gum" is reprinted from the Apr/May 2002 edition of *Storyworks* magazine. Copyright © 2002 by Scholastic, Inc. Reprinted by permission of Scholastic, Inc.

The Animal Thieves

Selling Illegal Pets Is Big Business

"The Animal Thieves" is reprinted from the Jan 2002 edition of *Storyworks* magazine. Copyright © 2002 by Scholastic, Inc. Reprinted by permission of Scholastic, Inc.

His name is Anson Wong, and he was one of the world's most dangerous thieves. He didn't rob banks or steal jewels. He stole animals from the wild—endangered and deadly animals. His specialty was the Komodo dragon, the world's largest land lizard. Wong earned millions of dollars selling his stolen animals to collectors around the world.

Wildlife experts celebrated last December when Wong was finally caught and put in jail. But animal smuggling remains a huge—and growing—problem around the world. "There are people in the United States and around the world who want to own exotic animals as pets," says Craig Hoover, an expert who works for the World Wildlife Fund. "As long as there are people willing to pay thousands of dollars for these animals, there will be people like Anson Wong willing to smuggle the animals out of the wild."

Dozens of different bird and reptile species are the victims of this illegal business. Endangered breeds of parrots, rare giant lizards and tortoises, and deadly snakes are especially popular with collectors.

Smugglers steal the animals or eggs from native habitats like jungles and rain forests. They then sneak them into countries where they can be sold as pets. Their smuggling methods are often cruel.

"They pack snakes and lizards into suitcases and drug birds before stuffing them into tires or tennis ball cans," says Hoover.

"These people will do anything." Of course, many animals die during their journeys.

This business has hurt many animal populations. "Thieves will go into a rain forest and steal hundreds of eggs from a single area," says Hoover. For a species already threatened or endangered, this kind of theft can be devastating.

Animal smuggling endangers humans, as well. Often someone will buy an exotic animal without having any idea how to care for it. Every year, for example, dozens of people in the United States are bitten by deadly snakes that were illegally sold as pets. One Florida man died last year from a cobra bite.

"This is an evil business," says Don Bruning, a bird specialist who works at the Wildlife Conservation Society in New York City. "It's wonderful that people are interested in unusual animals. But no one should be selling endangered or dangerous animals. And no matter how much money a person has to spend, they should never be able to buy a priceless part of our natural world."

Girls on Strike!

Harriet Hanson was eleven when she first walked through the gates of the giant mill at Lowell, Massachusetts. She had loved school, but her mother needed extra money. So like hundreds of other girls, Harriet took a job as a "bobbin girl" in the spinning room at one of Lowell's huge fabric mills. The windows were nailed shut and the room was hot and damp. Her wage was a dollar a week. Like the others, Harriet pinned up her hair to make sure it didn't get caught in the machinery. Then she faced her machine, reminding herself to be careful about where she put her fingers. Dozens of girls a year were injured by the dangerous machinery.

Mill owners convinced themselves that they were helping children build character through hard work. They fired men and replaced them with women and children, who worked for lower wages. Most girls stood up all day. They had a 15-minute break for breakfast and another 30-minute break at noon.

In the 1830s, the mill women and girls began to stand up for themselves, organizing strikes for more pay and shorter hours. In 1836, the workers at Harriet's mill began planning a strike. Because the company controlled virtually every part of a mill girl's life, it took

> HARRIET TOOK A JOB AS A "BOBBIN GIRL" IN THE SPINNING ROOM AT ONE OF LOWELL'S HUGE FABRIC MILLS. THE WINDOWS WERE NAILED SHUT AND THE ROOM WAS HOT AND DAMP. HER WAGE WAS A DOLLAR A WEEK.

courage to even think of "turning out," as they called striking. For weeks, Harriet listened as girls and women discussed just that, and then finally made the decision to strike.

On the strike day, as the signal to stop working was passed around, workers from the upper floors spilled out into the street, chanting. The mill was shut down. But girls in Harriet's spinning room remained frozen in place. What would the company do to them? What if they lost their jobs? Harriet was disgusted. For long minutes, the women stood at their looms, whispering among themselves. Finally, Harriet stood up. "I am going to turn out whether anyone else does or not."

With that, she marched toward the door. In the next moment she heard a great shuffling of feet. The entire floor had lined up behind her. Everyone was turning out.

Years later, as an adult, Harriet fought against slavery and became the first woman to testify before Congress in favor of the right of women to vote. But she often reminisced about that day in Lowell. "As I looked back on the long line that followed me," she later wrote, "I was more proud than I have ever been since."

"Girls on Strike" is reprinted from the Nov/Dec 2001 edition of *Storyworks* magazine.

The Smuggler

A Folktale From the Middle East

A clever smuggler led a donkey burdened with bundles of straw to the border between two lands. The inspector at the border eyed the donkey's bundles with suspicion.

"You must allow me to search your bundles!" the inspector said. "I think that you have hidden a valuable treasure that you wish to sell at the market. If so, you must pay me a border fee!"

"Search as you wish," said the man. "If you find something other than straw, I will pay whatever fee you ask."

The inspector pulled apart the straw bundles until there was straw in the air, straw on the ground, straw, straw, straw all around. Yet not a valuable thing in the straw was found.

"You are a clever smuggler!" said the inspector. "I am certain that you are hiding something. Yet so carefully have you covered it, I have not discovered it. Go!"

The man crossed the border with his donkey. The suspicious inspector looked on with a scowl.

The next day, the man came back to the border with a donkey burdened with straw. Once again the inspector pulled apart the bundles. There was straw in the air, straw on the ground, straw, straw, straw all around.

"Not one valuable thing have I found!" the exasperated inspector said. "Go!"

The man and the donkey went across the border. "Bah!" cried the inspector once again, scowling.

The next day and the next day, for ten years, the man came to the border with a donkey burdened with straw. Each day the inspector searched his bundles, but he found nothing.

Finally, the inspector retired. Even as an old man, he could not stop thinking about that clever smuggler. One day as he walked through the marketplace, still trying to solve the mystery at the border, he muttered, "I am certain that man was smuggling something. Perhaps I should have looked more carefully in the donkey's mouth. Or he could have hidden something between the hairs on the donkey's tail!"

As he mumbled to himself, he noticed a familiar face in the crowd. "You!" he exclaimed. "I know you! You were the man who came to the border every day with a donkey burdened with straw. Come and speak with me!"

When the man walked toward him, the old inspector said, "Admit it! You were smuggling something across the border, weren't you?" The man nodded and grinned.

"Aha!" said the old inspector. "Just as I suspected. You were sneaking something to market! Tell me what it was! What were you smuggling? Tell me, if you can."

"Donkeys," said the man.

"The Smuggler" from *Wisdom Tales From Around the World* by Heather Forest (August House, 1996).

The Talkative Turtle

A Wisdom Tale From Ancient India

Long ago in India, there lived a turtle who was always talking. His endless chatter annoyed the creatures who shared the pond, and they avoided him. He spent his days mumbling to himself as he climbed in and out of the water.

One day, two visiting geese landed along the shore. The turtle admired their sleek feathers, and spent many hours praising their beauty. At last, to avoid the turtle's ceaseless chatter, the geese prepared to fly off to another pond. "Take me with you!" cried the turtle. "I am lonely here, and you are fine company."

"How can we do such a thing?" asked the birds. "You cannot fly."

"Nothing is impossible," said the turtle. "I will think of a plan."

To the amusement of the geese, the turtle said, "It is quite simple. First, let us find a long, strong stick. Each of you can hold one end of it in your beak. I will then bite hard in the middle. When you fly up together, I will cling to the center of the stick with my strong mouth. That way you can carry me over the trees."

The geese replied, "What a ridiculous idea! You could fall to your death!"

The turtle protested, "I will not fall. My mouth is strong. I will hold on tightly."

"Your mouth is strong from endless talking," squawked the geese "You will be safe only if you can keep your mouth shut."

Indignantly, the turtle replied, "You think that I cannot keep quiet, but I can. I know when to be silent and when to speak. Admit it. My idea is excellent. Let me try my invention and fly with you."

"Very well," said the geese. "But we cannot guarantee your safety on this journey."

"Then go and get the stick," ordered the turtle. "You'll see how quiet I can be when silence is important."

The geese flew off and returned with a long, strong stick. They both took an end in their beaks. The turtle clamped his mouth onto the middle. As the geese beat their wings and flew into the air, the dangling turtle went up too.

Soaring high above the trees, they were a vision to behold. Some children at play looked up and noticed the strange trio. "Look! Look!" cried one child. "Two geese are carrying a turtle on a stick!"

Another child chimed in, "What clever birds! They thought of a way to carry turtles!"

Another cheered, "Good thinking, geese!"

The turtle heard the children's voices. Their words infuriated him. He fumed, "They should be complimenting me for this fine plan, not the geese." Outraged, the turtle exploded with sound.

"It was my idea!" he sputtered, as he tumbled to the ground.

Reprinted from the November/December 1998 edition of *Storyworks* magazine.

Wild Wolf Comeback

For years, there were no wolves left in Yellowstone National Park. Now, gray wolves are prowling the park again.

Where the Wolves Wander

The wolf packs are back! In the past 10 years, the number of wolf packs in Yellowstone National Park has grown. That has meant big changes in the park's ecology, or relationship among plants, animals, and their surroundings.

Packs in the Park

Until 1995, gray wolves had disappeared from Yellowstone. One reason why they died off is that humans hunted them. Then, in 1995, scientists brought in 14 wolves from Canada. The scientists wanted wolves to be part of the wildlife in the park again. Today, about 130 wolves roam, or wander around, Yellowstone, in 13 packs.

Food Chain

With wolves prowling Yellowstone again, what happens to other living things there? Wolves are at the top of the food chain (see graphic below), which means no other animal hunts them. But the meat-eating wolves hunt elk. Before the wolves made a comeback at Yellowstone, there were about 19,000 elk at the park. Today, there are about 11,000. Some experts think the elk population dropped because the wolves are preying on them.

These experts say that fewer elk is good news for trees. The elk eat young willow, aspen, and cottonwood trees. With fewer elk, these trees grow to their full size.

"Wolves are at the top of it all here," says Douglas W. Smith, a wolf expert at Yellowstone. "They change the conditions for everything else."

It is still too early to know the full effects of the wolves' return to Yellowstone. "Ten years is not that long a time to measure the effects of the wolves," says Smith. One thing is certain: The experts will be watching closely.

Follow the Yellowstone Food Chain

A food chain shows how animals are connected to each other through what they eat.

willow tree → **elk** → **gray wolf**

Trees are food for elk and other animals.

Elk are food for wolves.

Wolves are at the top of the food chain. No other animal in Yellowstone eats them.

Finding the Giant Squid

In many movies and stories, the giant squid is a scary monster. Now, scientists have found a real live one deep in the sea!

Super Squid!

It has eyes the size of basketballs. Its eight arms are covered with suckers. But it's not a monster—it's a giant squid. Now, scientists from Japan have photos of this creature in the deep sea.

"We believe this is the first time a grown giant squid was captured on camera in its natural habitat," said Kyoichi Mori, one of the scientists.

Fishing for Squid

Giant squid live deep in the ocean, where no light reaches. This makes them hard to find. Until now, experts could only study dead or sick ones that washed up on shore or were snagged by fishing boats.

To see a live squid, Mori and his team followed sperm whales, which eat giant squid. Then, they sunk a long line with a camera on the end into the sea. Also attached to the line were hooks and bait, such as shrimp.

The enormous, or very big, purple-colored creature got hooked. It later got free, but not before the camera had snapped 550 photos.

New Knowledge

The photos give us clues about how the giant squid swims and catches prey, or the animals it eats. Experts used to think giant squid might move slowly. But they have learned that this supersize squid is fast! Now that scientists know how to find giant squid, there will be plenty more to learn.

> It has eyes the size of basketballs. Its eight arms are covered with suckers. But it's not a monster—it's a giant squid.

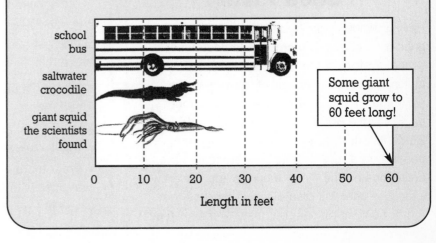

Sizing Up the Giant Squid

The giant squid found by the scientists was 25 feet long. How big is that? Check out the graph.

school bus
saltwater crocodile
giant squid the scientists found

Some giant squid grow to 60 feet long!

0   10   20   30   40   50   60
Length in feet

"Finding the Giant Squid" is reprinted from the 12/5/05 edition of *Scholastic News*. Copyright © 2005 by Scholastic, Inc. Reprinted by permission of Scholastic, Inc.

SUPERSIZE...to Go

Order a McDonald's Super Size soda soon, and you will likely walk away with a smaller drink. McDonald's, the largest fast-food restaurant chain in the world, will discontinue its Super Size soft drinks and french fries by the end of the year.

The decision comes at a time when extra-big portions of food are being linked to an epidemic of overweight Americans. Many nutrition experts believe that Americans eat too much. Super Size options, they argue, encourage that habit.

McDonald's says its decision to cut the Super Size is not about health arguments, but to streamline their menu. Still, the move has shone a light on the issue of portion size, which many experts say is key to healthy eating.

Dr. George Blackburn, an expert in nutrition at Harvard Medical School, says that Americans—including kids—need to cut down on the portions they eat.

"Kids should look at their hand as a serving size, whether it's a liquid or a solid," Dr. Blackburn said. "A fist or hand serving size is enough of that food to eat at one time."

A Health Concern

Health experts say that overeating and a lack of exercise have caused Americans to gain too much weight. Being overweight is linked to serious health problems including heart disease, type 2 diabetes, and some forms of cancer. A new study from the U.S. Department of Health and Human Services found that poor diet and physical inactivity may soon overtake tobacco as the leading preventable cause of death in the U.S.

A Serving Size Is Enough

Getting a handle on how much makes up a normal serving size is an important part of eating balanced meals. Health experts say many Americans simply don't know what's enough when it comes to food. Food portions have increased drastically in recent decades. In 1950, a single serving of Coca-Cola came in one size—a 6.5-ounce bottle. Today, Americans gulp down 20-ounce bottles of Coke at one time, thinking it is a single serving. Actually, 20 ounces is two-and-a-half servings.

It's About Choices

A balanced diet also means limiting foods—like candy and soda—that are high in unneeded fats and sugars. Healthy eating doesn't mean giving up those treats altogether. But health experts say cutting down on them is a must. One way is to choose healthier options, like fruits and vegetables, during meals and snacks (see Healthy Choices).

Everyone's Fight

Everyone needs to know about proper nutrition. Eating a balanced diet and staying fit helps the brain work better, increases energy levels, and can even help guard against health concerns like acne.

But remember: Eating healthy is not about how you look, it's about how you feel. It's about making informed choices to become the healthiest version of you.

Good Taste

Having healthier choices for school lunch is no good if no one eats them. The largest public school system in the nation—New York City—is looking for an executive chef to oversee the school lunch menu. It's a big job. New York serves some 800,000 school meals a day! Students seem to agree that a food guru is needed. At a recent taste-test, students gave selections on the menu a poor grade. The new executive chef will create school lunches that are not only nutritious, but taste and look good.

Healthy Choices

It doesn't take big changes to make healthy choices at meal or snack time. Health experts offer these tips for achieving a more balanced diet.

- Skip the soda. Order water with your hamburger and fries.
- Having a snack attack? Grab some fresh vegetables and dip them in low-fat dip.
- Order more colorful toppings. Load up that slice of pizza with veggies.
- Still feeling hungry after dinner? Have some fruit—it's very sweet and full of vitamins.

Kids Need More Zzzs

According to a new study, kids are not getting enough sleep.

Do you drink caffeinated beverages every day, or watch TV right before you go to bed? You may want to put a lid on the soda and turn off the tube if you want a good night's sleep.

A recent poll of sleep habits in the U.S. has found that American kids are not getting enough sleep. Experts blame two major culprits for the problem: caffeine and television.

Not Enough Shut-eye

The National Sleep Foundation poll found that kids up to age 10 are getting an average of 9.5 hours of sleep each night. They need 10 or 11 hours of sleep. This can add up to a sleep deficit of about 10 hours a week.

Sleep experts say that a lack of shut-eye can hamper a kid's ability to focus, which can make it difficult to learn. It may also make a kid more accident-prone.

"Sleep is a vital asset for a child's health and overall development, learning, and safety," says the Sleep Foundation's Richard L. Gelula.

Why So Wide-awake?

Kids who drink at least one beverage with caffeine in it per day sleep a half hour less each night than kids who do not drink caffeine at all, according to the poll. The survey also showed that kids who have TVs in their bedrooms generally go to sleep about 20 minutes later than those without TVs in their rooms.

Watching TV in bed is part of the reason sixth-grader Anthony Alvarado of California is tired in school.

Anthony told the Sacramento Bee that he hits the hay around 11:30 p.m. and watches TV in his room until he falls asleep. he gets up around 7 am. for school. "I feel like a zombie," Anthony said.

Do You Get Enough Sleep?

How do you know if you're getting enough sleep?

One expert says a good way to find out is to go to bed on a weekend night at the same time you would go to bed on a weeknight. If you get up the next morning after you normally would to go to school, you're probably not getting enough sleep during the week.

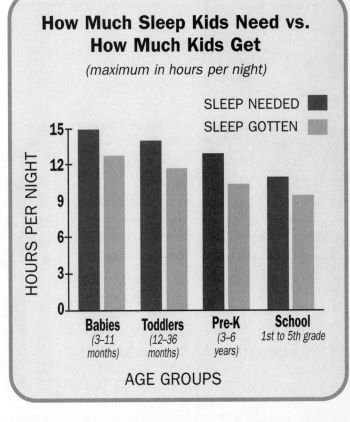

How Much Sleep Kids Need vs. How Much Kids Get

(maximum in hours per night)

SLEEP NEEDED

SLEEP GOTTEN

HOURS PER NIGHT

AGE GROUPS: Babies *(3–11 months)*, Toddlers *(12–36 months)*, Pre-K *(3–6 years)*, School *1st to 5th grade*

Great Gliders!

I work in the rain forests of Asia. Many animals there glide from tree to tree. So when I want to take pictures of them, I have to climb the trees myself!

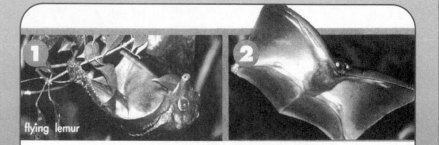

flying lemur

Flying Lemurs Glide!

The flying lemur glides to escape enemies and find leaves to eat. It has wings of skin. To glide, it leaps and opens its wings. They catch air. To land, it grabs on to tree trunks with its sharp claws.

Flying lemurs are nocturnal, too. Once, I stayed up in a tree all night long to get a photo of a nocturnal animal!

Frogs Glide!

webbed feet

Wallace's flying frog

I bring lights with me when I take pictures of this kind of frog. That's because it is nocturnal, or active at night.

This frog glides when it wants to get away from enemies like monkeys. It also glides to places with lots of insects to eat.

First, it leaps from a tree. Then, it glides through the air. Its big, webbed feet help it go. They catch the air, like kites.

The frog's sticky toes help it land. The frog can land right on floppy leaves and not fall off!

Snakes Glide!

I think all of the gliding animals are cool. I have a favorite, though. It's a snake! Like the other animals, it glides to get away from enemies. It also glides to look for tasty lizards to eat.

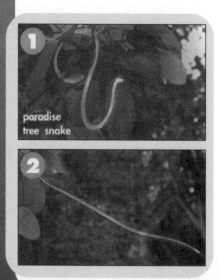

paradise tree snake

First, it hangs from a branch. Then, it pushes off into the air. It sucks in its body and spreads out its ribs. It becomes flat and flies through the air.

To land, it throws itself on a branch and wraps itself around, like a rope. Picture that!

Too Warm?

Look ahead to the year 2050. Will Florida get too hot, forcing panthers to prowl northward? Could glaciers in the Arctic melt away, leaving polar bears clinging to the last bits of ice?

Although no one can predict the future, a new study recently found that rising temperatures around the world could harm or kill thousands of species by the time you are in your 50s. Warming weather could stretch out summers and cut winters short. Climate change could also force animals to migrate to areas where they may not be able to survive.

"Wild animals depend on climate," says scientist Lee Hannah, who helped write the study. "When their climate changes, they move, or else they will usually die. And our climate is changing."

Up North, Down South

Over the last 100 years, the average temperature on Earth has risen by 1 degree Fahrenheit. That may not sound like much, but it alarms scientists, because it's the fastest the earth has warmed up in 1,000 years.

Animals in the world's polar regions are already feeling the heat. Some scientists think that Arctic sea ice is melting at a rate of 10 percent per decade. That's bad news for the 22,000 polar bears living near the North Pole. The bears use the ice as a hunting platform. They walk on ice sheets to get closer to swimming seals, their favorite food.

Arctic seals also depend on sea ice—it's where they rest, give birth, and molt, or shed their fur, each year. As the ice disappears, some seals die or move onto land. As a result, many polar bears end up starving, as well.

On the opposite side of the world, sea ice in Antarctica is also shrinking: 20 percent of it has melted over the last 50 years. This has forced penguins to waddle to colder areas closer to the South Pole. Penguins raise their young on sheets of sea ice. Some penguins also eat krill, small shrimplike creatures that feed on algae that clings to the ice. As the ice melts, the krill population slips away—and so do the penguins' chances for survival.

What's Going On?

Earth's climate often changes due to natural causes. Many scientists think that the recent climate change is part of this natural pattern.

However, many other scientists think that human activity may be to blame for global warming. People use fossil fuels such as oil, coal, and gas to heat their homes and run cars and factories. The burning fuels release carbon dioxide, a natural gas, into the air. Carbon dioxide traps heat in the atmosphere. Too much carbon dioxide can trap more heat than the earth needs, causing temperatures to rise.

Scientists hope that new inventions and laws designed to reduce air pollution can cut down on global warming. They also hope that, by setting aside more open land for wild animals, people can protect species that may be forced to migrate.

"No one can tell what will happen in the future," says Lee Hannah. "With hope, these predictions won't come true."

"Too Warm" by Fiona McCormack is reprinted from the March 1, 2004 edition of *Scholastic News*. Copyright © 2004 by Scholastic, Inc. Reprinted by permission of Scholastic, Inc.

Spiders' Spinning Secrets

Scientists are close to unraveling the secret wrapped up in silk.

Which frightens you more—a scary ghost story or a spider dangling from the ceiling? Spiders scare many people, but most spiders are harmless. In fact, spiders have a secret that may be very helpful to humans.

The secret is that spiders spin silk that is stronger than any other known material. Spider silk is so strong, say scientists, that a web woven of spider silk the thickness of a pencil could stop a jet in mid-flight!

The strength of spiders' silk has stumped humans for over a century. But scientists have recently come one step closer to unraveling the spider's secret. This discovery is expected to help humans figure out how to make artificial spider silk.

The Power of Silk

Spider silk is the material that spiders use to build webs and catch food. They also use it to climb and to protect their eggs.

Spiders have been spinning silk for about 380 million years—that's 150 million years before the first dinosaurs roamed the earth!

Although the appearance and size of each kind of spider varies greatly, all spiders have the ability to spin silk.

Now humans want to learn how to spin silk like spiders. Over the last 10 years, scientists have been working to make artificial spider silk, but they haven't created anything as strong as the real stuff.

Learning how to copy spider silk could help humans because of the material's unique combination of strength and stretch. Spider silk is tougher than steel and more flexible than rubber.

Why not use real spider silk? Raising thousands of spiders to produce silk would be difficult. One problem is that spiders are territorial and don't like to be crowded. To solve this problem, they eat one another!

Solving the Silk Secret

A new finding is making scientists hopeful that they will soon solve the spiders' silk secret. Scientist David Kaplan has figured out how spiders mix water and silk proteins in their bodies to create threads of silk.

"This finding is expected to help scientists copy the process spiders' bodies go through when they make silk," says Kaplan.

If scientists can do this, they should be able to figure out how to create artificial silk as strong as a spider's silk.

Think About It!

Spiders live in just about every habitat on earth because they have learned to adapt to different environments. For example, some spiders build tents that they use as retreats or hiding places to find shelter from rain or enemies.

"Spider silk is a science wonder," says Jeffrey Turner, whose company is working to make artificial silk.

Some of the products Turner's company may be able to improve with artificial silk include: lighter and tougher bulletproof vests, bridge cables that can withstand earthquakes, and car bumpers that resist dents.

Maybe spiders and cobwebs aren't so creepy after all!

So Many Spiders!

There are more than 30,000 known species of spiders. But scientists believe there may be 20,000 to 70,000 species that have not yet been discovered. Find out about some of the spider species below.

- **THE JUMPING SPIDER** can leap 10 to 40 times its body length. Jumping spiders feed on insects and other web-building spiders.

- **THE WOLF SPIDER** is a ground-dwelling, hunting spider. It has a short body and long, thick legs.

- **THE TARANTULA** is a large, hairy spider that lives in warm areas around the world. The biggest known tarantula had a leg span of about 13 inches.

A Lizard Tale

Most animals get bigger as they get older. Did you know that some iguanas can make themselves smaller?

These iguanas live on the Galapagos (ga-LA-pa-goes) Islands, off the coast of

Ecuador. When their food supply is low, the iguanas shrink. Why? The smaller they are, the less they need to eat.

Throughout the year, the iguanas forage, or search, for food. They eat small plants called algae (AL-jee). Sometimes, the Galapagos Islands are hit by a weather system called El Niño. This weather system brings heavy rainfall to the islands. The rainfall causes the

amount of algae to decrease. The iguanas then have much less to eat. If they stayed at their normal size, the iguanas would starve to death.

Experts found that the iguanas can shrink themselves by about three inches. This always happens during the food shortages caused by El Niño. One expert, Dr. Martin Wikelski, said, "They shrink to reach a body size where they can survive."

The experts learned something else: Once the weather and food supply return to normal, the iguanas go back to their normal size!

Amazing Changes

Iguanas aren't the only animals that can change their bodies to survive. Here are some others:

Chameleon—a lizard that can change its color to blend in with its surroundings. This allows the chameleon to hide from predators.

Puffer—a fish that can inflate its body to twice its size, like a balloon. It swallows water or air to take on the shape of a ball. A puffer does this to protect itself from its enemies.

Volcanic View

awaii is growing. The state of Hawaii is made up of a chain of islands. The biggest island is called Hawaii—and it's getting bigger and bigger every day.

The flow of lava from Kilauea (kee-lah-way-uh), the world's most active volcano, has added 544 acres of new land to it. Kilauea blew its top in 1983. It has been erupting ever since and shows no signs of stopping.

The volcano has lured millions of visitors a year to its edges. People are drawn to see nature in one of its most raw and ancient forms.

It's a Natural

It's no surprise that Kilauea is in Hawaii. Hawaii was formed by volcanoes. The Hawaiian Islands are at the end of a chain of volcanoes that began to form more than 70 million years ago. The volcanoes first erupted on the ocean floor. Over millions of years, hardened lava piled up and eventually rose above the sea surface.

Most of the state's active volcanoes, including Kilauea, are on the island of Hawaii, also known as the Big Island of Hawaii. Kilauea covers hundreds of square miles. Lava flows from several vents (holes) in the volcano.

Fireworks

The lava, smoke, and occasional small explosions that most visitors to Kilauea see, occur where rivers of lava reach the Pacific Ocean. Lava flows snake seaward above the ground and below it The lava reaches temperatures of more than 1,500 degrees Fahrenheit.

Steam is produced when lava and ocean water meet Steam-pressured explosions sometimes result, which can spray hot lava and basketball-size rocks hundreds of feet.

Lava Flow
Magma becomes lava once it leaves a volcano. Lava is very hot—1,500 degrees Fahrenheit!

Magma Pool
Magma collects in a pool in the surface of the earth. It breaks through the surface when pressure builds up.

Vents
Hot magma bursts through holes called vents. Ash, solid rocks, and gases also shoot out of vents.

Tourists must stay away from the newly created land near the water. The land is unstable and sometimes has volcanic debris falling on it.

Also, volcanoes create what is called "vog," or volcanic smog. The gas is a visible haze that results when chemicals from the volcano come into contact with air and sunlight. Winds weaken the gas, but it is thick near cracks in the ground and unhealthy to breathe.

During the last century, at least four people have been killed at Kilauea. In one case, a visitor stepped on new land at the ocean's edge, and the ground collapsed underneath him. A photographer was killed by falling debris. Earthquakes, which are common near volcanoes, have also claimed lives near Kilauea.

All in a Day's Work

In 1990, Kilauea buried an entire town called Kalapana. More than 200 homes were destroyed. Luckily, no one was hurt. One reason they were not harmed is that the United States Geological Service (USGS) watches Kilauea constantly. It is able to alert people to brewing danger.

Meanwhile, the oozing, red-hot lava and newly formed land wow even the scientists.

"This is just absolutely wild. It's got noise, it's got smell, it's got feel, touch…. It's just raw." said Don Swanson of the USGS. "It's a real rush."

The cool water also hardens the lava, creating the new land on Hawaii's edge. About 412 football fields would fit on the land formed since Kilauea began erupting 20 years ago.

Dangerous Terrain

Visitors to Hawaii Volcanoes National Park, where Kilauea is located, are strongly cautioned about the hazards that accompany volcanoes.

Not Enough Bees

Are you afraid of bees because they can sting you? Did you ever wish that these critters would just "BEE" gone? According to experts, that would be a disaster for our food supply. Bees help provide much of the food we eat. What's the big deal about bees?

While the buzz of bees may scare third graders, that buzz is music to a farmer's ears. Bees carry a sticky substance called pollen from flower to flower. The pollen helps flowers grow into fruits and vegetables (see diagram at right). "We couldn't grow crops without honeybees," says expert Gloria DeGrandi-Hoffman. Where have all the bees gone?

Since 1990, our nation's bees have been dying. One problem is mites. These tiny members of the spider family have killed many bees. Mites attack baby bees before the bees have a chance to grow.

Pesticides are another problem. Pesticides are chemicals that farmers spray on crops to keep pesky insects away. The chemicals sometimes kill bees. Farmers are now starting to use pesticides that are less harmful to bees.

So if you see a bee, be careful, but don't kill it. That busy bee's buzzing is helping to feed the world!

Bees Help Food Grow!

1. A bee takes pollen from the **ANTHER** of one flower.
2. The bee flies to a new flower and rubs the pollen on that flower's **STIGMA**.
3. The pollen travels down a tube called the **STYLE**, and ends up in the flower's **OVARY**.
4. Seeds form in the ovary. Fruit grows around these seeds.

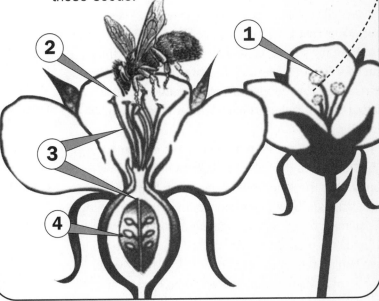

Sacajawea

A Teen Who Led the Way

Her name means "Bird Woman" in the language of her Shoshone tribe. Sacajawea [SACK-uh-juh-WEE-uh] was just 16 when she joined one of the most important expeditions in American history—Lewis and Clark's journey from the Mississippi River to the Pacific Ocean between 1803 and 1806.

In his historical novel about the event, author Joseph Bruchac imagines an older Sacajawea telling the story to her son, who had traveled with her as a baby. In this excerpt, she describes how she earned the explorers' respect.

I was quick to show them how I could be of use to them, even before the time came for me to help them speak with our people. Their canoes and the two big boats were filled with wonderful things of all sorts. They carried with them provisions of different kinds, including salted meat and food that had been dried in preparation for a long journey. But they did not have enough food with them to feed more than 20 hungry mouths. They needed to hunt to survive.

The two captains were fine hunters. In those first days of travel their talk was often of the animals they had been told about but had not yet seen.

They talked especially about the One Who Walks Like a Man. That is how our people always speak of the great bear, my son. If you do not show respect to the bear, he will not respect you. So it was that I worried when I heard the captains talk with excitement about hunting the grizzly bear. I hoped they would remember to respect him.

In the meantime, they brought in elk and buffalo, deer and beaver. It seemed a plentiful hunt. I knew, though, that the time would come when hunting would not be enough. High in the mountains, where our people live, animals would not be as numerous as they were in the lands we passed through at first. One day we would leave behind the great herds of buffalo. There would come a time when any animal would be hard to find.

We women had learned long ago how to find food other than the animals the men hunt.

I kept my eyes open. One evening, I saw something I had been looking for—a great pile of driftwood in a place where the earth seemed to be piled up on the bank of the river. I chose a strong driftwood stick and began thrusting it into the soft earth.

Where were you then? Do you not remember? You were right there with me in your cradleboard.

Soon I broke through one of the storage places in the ground made by the harvester mice. It was stuffed with a great mound of the round white roots that are the size of a man's finger. Those roots have a sweet taste and the mice gather them in great numbers.

By then Captain Lewis was watching me with such care that I was certain he would make markings that night about what I had done. I had never seen men spend so much of their time making those markings in the little bundles of white leaves sewed together, which I later learned were called journals. Those journals were as important to them as their own lives. But all that I could see in the lines the two captains drew were shapes that made no sense to me. Yes, my wise son, I know that you are able to write such talking lines and understand what the talking lines made by others say to you.

I thanked the little harvester mice and gave them a present from my pouch. The captains and all the men were very pleased when they tasted those roots. They ate all I had gathered and urged me to find more wherever I could. Then everyone sat around the fire, talking of that day's travel, and I sat with them.

Later, we came to a river, one that flowed strong with clear water. The two captains both looked at me that day as they made marks in their books. That river, they told me, now shared my name. It was now Bird Woman's River. I felt something then. I still cannot tell you whether I was proud, but I was touched that they had done this. It was strange to leave a part of myself with that river.

Rabbit and Tiger

A Vietnamese Folktale

Rabbit perched quietly at the forest's edge, cleaning her whiskers. She wanted very much to relax and take her afternoon nap, but she sensed that Tiger, the ruler of the forest, was near. "He could eat me up in one bite," she said to herself, shuddering at the thought.

When Rabbit was younger, she could have easily outrun Tiger. Now her muscles and joints had begun to ache, and Rabbit was feeling old and stiff.

"The only way I can keep from becoming Tiger's next meal is to outsmart him," she thought.

Rabbit spent the rest of the day trying to think up a way to outsmart Tiger. But the idea that kept coming to her made her whiskers quiver with fear.

At first Rabbit tried to talk herself out of such a dangerous plan, but at last she decided she had no other choice.

"I will try it out tomorrow," she said. "Otherwise, I must hide for the rest of my life and never nap in peace."

Bright and early the next morning, Rabbit set off for the forest along a trail that she knew Tiger would use. She had just sat down to wait when Tiger came strolling down the trail.

Tiger was surprised to have a handy meal waiting so willingly. He padded up to Rabbit and placed a huge paw on her back.

"I have enough room in my stomach for one last tasty morsel," he said, running his tongue over his whiskers. "How thoughtful of you to wait for me."

Rabbit sat quietly and said nothing, hoping her plan would work.

"What is wrong with you, Rabbit? I have always frightened you, as I frighten all the animals of the forest. Today you sit here and wait for me to gobble you up. Aren't you afraid of me?"

Rabbit felt the weight of his giant paw and hoped Tiger couldn't feel her trembling under it. "Afraid of you?" she said, trying to sound calm. "Why should I be afraid of you?"

"Because I am the ruler of the forest, that's why," huffed Tiger.

"That's not what I heard."

Tiger eyed Rabbit suspiciously. "What are you talking about?" he growled.

"All the animals of the forest got together for a special meeting while you were out hunting last night. Maybe that's why you haven't heard," said Rabbit, daring to look straight into his glowing amber eyes.

"Haven't heard what?" asked Tiger.

"That you are no longer the ruler of the forest," said Rabbit, slipping out from under the giant paw. "The animals have decided that I am the fiercest animal in the forest."

"A puny thing like you?" scoffed Tiger, opening his mouth wide enough to swallow her whole.

"I can prove it," said Rabbit, gulping at the sight of his sharp, gleaming teeth. "I will ride on your back as you go through the forest. That way you will see for yourself how terrified the animals are of me. If they are not, then you can make me your next meal."

Before Tiger had time to think, Rabbit hopped onto his back and urged him to move on.

Tiger slunk through the trees. As usual, every animal fled at his approach. But before they ran, they stopped to stare at Rabbit with wide-eyed amazement. Mistaking their looks of amazement for terror, Tiger thought, "Look at their frightened faces! Rabbit must indeed be the fiercest animal in the forest."

He sank to the ground at her feet. "Rabbit, forgive me for how I have behaved," he begged. "And if you can find it in your heart, spare my life."

"Very well," said Rabbit, quite pleased with how things were working out. "But because you have frightened me so in the past, you must promise to leave this part of the forest and never return."

Tiger agreed. From then on, Rabbit not only enjoyed her afternoon naps in peace, she won the admiration of the other animals for her cleverness.

"Rabbit and Tiger" retold by Virginia Castleman is reprinted from *Highlights for Children*, May 1999 issue.

The Leopard and the Rat

A Story From Ghana

Once upon a time, all the animals lived in a big forest. There was plenty of food, so the animals were very happy.

One day as Rat was looking for food, he heard a cry from far away. "Help, help! Oh, please help me!" the voice said.

"Who is crying like that?" Rat asked himself. "I must go and see who it is. I do hope I can help."

He went nearer and nearer to the cry. He still heard, "Help, help! Please help me!"

Then he came to a deep, dark hole. He looked down, and at the bottom he saw Leopard.

"Oh, help me, please. Please help me," cried Leopard.

"Oh! You are Leopard!" said Rat. "I fear that if I help you out, you will eat me."

"No! No!" exclaimed Leopard. "How could I eat the one who helps me? I would never do that, I promise."

"Are you sure you will not harm me?" asked Rat.

"Surely, I will not harm you," Leopard said. "In fact, I will reward you."

"All right," said Rat. "I will help you. Stop crying. I will be back in a moment."

Rat went to cut some vines. He wove them together to make a strong rope. He tied one end of the rope to a tree and dropped the other end into the hole.

"Here you are," he said. "Use this rope to climb out of the hole."

"Oh, thank you very much," said Leopard as she grabbed the rope.

As Leopard was climbing, Rat kept encouraging her.

"Try hard. There you are. You are doing well. Try harder. Very good, you will soon be out." With great difficulty Leopard climbed out of the hole. As soon as she came out, she grabbed Rat.

"I must eat you for my dinner," she said. "I am very hungry, so I cannot let you go."

"Oh, please do not eat me," cried Rat. "You promised not to harm me. I have little children at home. If you eat me, they will starve."

"I don't care about your children," growled Leopard. "In fact I would like to eat them, too, because you are too small for my dinner."

"Please let me go," cried Rat. But Leopard continued, "I am a respected animal in the forest. My hide is displayed by chiefs and kings. If I let you go, you will tell the rest of the animals that you, a common rat, saved my life."

"I will not tell any of them," cried Rat.

Suddenly they saw somebody coming. It was Ananse the spider, walking thoughtfully.

When he got to them, he asked Leopard, "Why is Rat crying so much?"

But Rat spoke up. "I helped Leopard out of this hole, and now she wants to eat me up."

"Liar!" shouted Ananse. "How could you, a common rat, a small animal like you, help a strong animal like Leopard out of this hole?"

"It's true," said Rat. "I helped her with this rope. I—"

"Enough of your lies!" yelled Ananse. "Leopard, why don't you just get back into the hole and let me see what really happened."

Eager to prove that Rat was a liar, Leopard jumped back into the hole before thinking. Ananse quickly pulled out the rope and cut it into pieces.

Then Ananse called into the hole, "Leopard, can you hear me?" "Yes, loud and clear," replied Leopard.

"All right, show me how you climbed out of the hole," Ananse said.

"Where is the rope? I cannot climb out without the rope," Leopard said.

"Aha," said Ananse. "So Rat did help you. Since this is how you repaid the one who was kind to you, you must get out the same way you got in."

"Thank you so much, Ananse," said Rat. Then he ran home as fast as he could to his little children.

"The Leopard and the Rat" retold by Mary Abena Griffin is reprinted from *Highlights for Children*, April 2001 issue.

Bug Business Crawls With Success

What would your mother say if you wanted to use her dishes to bake bugs in the oven? In Salisbury, Mo., Randy Meissen not only bakes bugs in the oven, his mother encourages it. Why? Because Randy is the owner of Meissen Entomology Co., which collects, resin-casts, and sells bugs for profit.

Randy's hobby turned into a business during his freshman year of high school under a Supervised Agricultural Experience Project with Future Farmer's of America (FFA). His advisor taught entomology and offered to buy insects for the Agriculture Department.

Randy spent the summer collecting sixty specimens. The collection was mounted and sold for $2.00 per bug.

Finding bugs is easy living on a farm; however, preserving them was a trial-and-error process. When he finally found a suitable resin-casting compound it came without instructions. His first attempts were, as Randy puts it, "a disaster."

"I baked the bugs in my mom's oven, ruining her dishes and a lot of specimens before I got it right."

Randy faced a couple of big challenges early in his business. In the summer of 1997 mice destroyed the entire summer's worth of collecting, chewing through 700 specimens, and nasty weather in 1998 prevented filling orders because of low populations of a specific moth species.

But the biggest hurdle of all was credibility.

"Teachers were hesitant to place orders with a student. I overcame this by building a reputation," Randy remembers.

After participating in a variety of state competitions in entomological identification, Randy received an Agri-Entrepreneurship Award from the Kaufman Center for Entrepreneurial Leadership. He listened to agricultural teachers talk about their needs for products for their entomology classes. This led to sales with the Clopton FFA chapter and his school's science department.

By recognizing opportunities, acting on ideas, and setting systematic plans to reach goals, Randy gained valuable experience and earned money for college.

In four years, Meissen Entomology Co. has expanded from word-of-mouth advertising to a catalog and website serving customers nationwide.

In November, he was a finalist in the National FFA Agricultural Sales and Service Proficiency Awards and recently placed third in the National Future Business Leaders of America.

Randy says, "Recognition and entrepreneurial distinction help build business." Randy will maintain his business while earning a degree in biochemistry at Rice University before attending medical school.

"People used to tease me about bugs, but I guess I'm the one laughing now," he says.

A laugh he certainly has earned.

You can bug Randy at his Web site— http://insects.virtualave.net.

"Bug Business Crawls with Success" by Jean Perry is reprinted from *Kids' Wall Street Journal*, Fall 1998 issue.

Popcorn Capital of the World

Poppin Facts: Popcorn probably originated in Mexico.

The oldest popcorn ears found are about 5,600 years old, in the Bat Cave in New Mexico.

Served by Colonial housewives with sugar and cream for breakfast—the first "puffed" breakfast eaten by Europeans.

First popcorn "machine" invented by Charlie Cretors in 1885.

During the Depression, popcorn (5 to 10 cents a bag) was one of the few luxuries many families could afford.

In 1945 Percy Spencer discovered that popcorn popped when placed under microwave energy. This led to the birth of the microwave oven.

During World War II, sugar was sent overseas for U.S. troops, leaving little sugar for candy. Thus Americans ate three times as much popcorn as usual.

In the early 1950s popcorn went into a slump when television became popular and movie attendance dropped. Popcorn resurged when people began eating the tasty treat at home.

Source: The Popcorn Institute. Check out the Web site at www.popcorn.org.

Top Popcorn Growers in the World

Indiana
Illinois
Nebraska
Ohio
Kentucky
Kansas
Missouri
Iowa
Michigan

Pop On In!

Popcorn is big business in Marion, Ohio. The town exports 18 million pounds of popcorn each year and hosts the Marion Popcorn Festival, which draws more than 200,000 people. Visitors come to hear the big-name entertainers, watch the parade, sample the 50 flavors of popcorn and participate in the various popcorn activities.

Marion is also home of the Wyandot Popcorn Museum, the world's largest collection of antique popcorn poppers.

Americans consume 17.3 billion quarts of popped popcorn, and the average American eats about 68 quarts each year.

While other businesses failed in the 1930s, the popcorn business thrived. An Oklahoma farmer who went broke when his bank failed, started selling popcorn near a theater. After a couple of years, he was able to buy back three of the farms he'd lost.

"Popcorn Capital of the World" is reprinted from *Kids' Wall Street Journal*, Fall 1998 issue.

The Sixth Sense

Can animals predict natural disasters?

December 26th was a beautiful, sunny day in Sri Lanka's Yala National Park, and hundreds of tourists on the park's beaches were sunning themselves. But among the park's elephants, the mood was hardly peaceful. In the middle of giving their midmorning rides, the animals trumpeted wildly and ran up a hill, away from the ocean. Other elephants broke their sturdy chains and chased after them to higher ground. The keepers could tell their animals were worried about something. But what could it be?

Suddenly, a 30-foot wave—the Indian Ocean tsunami—crashed into the coast. The wall of water flooded much of the park, crumbling buildings and drowning almost four thousand people. But instead of being swept away, the elephants stood safely on their hill.

Scientists have long suspected that animals sense natural disasters sooner than humans do. Before an earthquake, chickens often stop laying eggs, and snakes come out of hibernation to flee. As the recent tsunami sped toward land, flamingos fled low-lying ground, and tigers rushed into their shelters. Even in the hardest hit areas of Southeast Asia, survivors found few dead animals. Many people wondered: Did the animals know something we didn't? "Some animals have an acute sense of hearing and smell," says Alan Rabinowitz, of the Wildlife Conservation Society in New York City. "It allows them to sense something coming far before humans can."

Vibrations from within the earth may have given the elephants in Sri Lanka a sign that disaster was about to strike. Indeed, a gigantic earthquake under the Indian Ocean, more than 700 miles away from Yala Park, triggered the tsunami. Because the vibrations in the ground travel much faster than an ocean wave, the elephants may have felt the disturbance well before the tsunami slammed into the coast.

But can the "sixth sense" of animals help us predict disasters? A few scientists are calling for a system to track phone reports of strange behavior in people's pets. But many experts are skeptical. Because we can never be sure what an animal is thinking, they argue, we can't know if a dog is barking because of an earthquake or just because it wants to be fed. "Animals react to so many things—being hungry, defending their territories, predators," says Andy Michael, a geophysicist at the United States Geological Survey. "It's hard to get an advanced warning signal."

"The Sixth Sense" by Barry Rust is reprinted from the April/May 2005 edition of *Storyworks* magazine. Copyright © 2005 by Scholastic, Inc. Reprinted by permission of Scholastic, Inc.

Shark Attack Mystery

Did a 15-foot tiger shark really attack surfer Bethany Hamilton by mistake?

Two years ago, when world-class surfer Bethany Hamilton was attacked by a shark, the incident made news around the world. The 13-year-old was lying on her surfboard in the calm waters off Kauai, Hawaii. Then, a 15-foot tiger shark appeared without a splash of warning, grabbing Bethany's left arm and tearing it off. Just as suddenly, the shark disappeared. Bethany paddled to shore with one arm, losing 70 percent of the blood in her body. By the time she reached the hospital, she was nearly dead.

But Bethany didn't just survive—a few months later she was back in the water, surfing and winning tournaments. When she's not competing, Bethany travels the world sharing her story, inspiring people with her strength and spirit.

Bethany's story is incredible. But to many, the most incredible part is that Bethany lived to tell it. Why did the shark let go, they wonder, when it could have easily eaten the young surfer?

The answer, according to many scientists, is that the shark attacked Bethany by mistake. Sharks, even "man-eaters" like great whites and tigers, usually feast on fat, fleshy seals and sea lions. Humans, by comparison, are lean and bony. Many researchers believe that some sharks—especially the young and inexperienced ones—make mistakes when they hunt. When the shark catches hold of a swimmer or surfer, it quickly realizes that its prey isn't going to make a satisfying meal. So it lets go, as the tiger shark did when it attacked Bethany.

Bolstering this theory is the fact that shark attacks are rare, even in the waters off the coast of California, which are teeming with sharks. Hundreds of thousands of people surf and play in those waters each year, yet there have been fewer than 80 shark attacks there in the last 50 years. Only seven of those attacks have been fatal. "If people were a natural prey of sharks, we'd be getting 10 attacks an hour," says biologist Steve Kaiser, a leading shark researcher.

Bethany agrees that sharks are not especially interested in humans. Since her accident, she has encountered three sharks, including a 5-foot hammerhead that swam directly under her board without even looking at her.

Still, Bethany takes extra precautions. She no longer surfs early in the morning or at dusk, prime feeding times for sharks. And she now surfs on a board emblazoned with bold black and white stripes. She thinks the stripes look cool, but sharks don't, since the same pattern is found on some poisonous sea creatures. "The sharks are way scared of those stripes," Bethany says.

"Shark Attack Mystery" by Barry Rust is reprinted from the Jan 2006 edition of *Storyworks* magazine. Copyright © 2006 by Scholastic, Inc. Reprinted by permission of Scholastic, Inc.

Publisher Information

Benchmark Education
629 Fifth Avenue, Pelham, NY 10803, 1-877-236-2465, www.benchmarkeducation.com
Range of short-leveled nonfiction guided reading texts; content related topics; theme sets; readers' theater primary and intermediate levels

Candlewick Press
2067 Massachusetts Avenue, Cambridge, MA 02140, 1-800-526-0275, www.candlewick.com
Various children's books for the guided and independent reading and literature study groups

Capstone Press
151 Good Councel Drive, P.O. Box 669, Mankato, NM 56002-0669, 1-800-747-4992, www.capstone-press.com
Wide range of nonfiction books for guided and independent reading and classroom library; intervention high interest selections; graphic-novel style nonfiction history and biography; theme sets

Edmark
Riverdeep, Inc., 100 Pine Street, Suite 1900, San Francisco, CA 94111, 1-415-659-2000 www.riverdeep.net
Software programs in language arts and math

ETA/Cuisenaire
500 Greenview Court, Vernon Hills, IL 60061-1862, 1-800-875-9643, www.etacuisenaire.com
Fiction and nonfiction books for guided reading and independent books; series books; theme sets; content related topics

Harcourt Brace
6277 Sea Harbor Drive, Orlando, FL 32887, 1-407-345-2000, www.harcourt.com
Classroom library book collections for independent reading; Range of leveled content related nonfiction books for guided reading

Heinemann Classroom
6277 Harbor Drive, Orlando, FL 32887, 1-888-454-2279, www.heinemannclassroom.com
Range of nonfiction books for guided and independent reading; includes many content related subject titles; biographies

Houghton Mifflin Company
222 Berkeley Street, Boston, MA 02116, 1-617-351-5000, www.hmco.com
Range of leveled guided reading books

Mondo Publishing
980 Avenue of the Americas, New York, NY 10018, 1-888-886-6636, www.mondopub.com
Variety of fiction and nonfiction guided reading books; short chapter books for guided and independent reading or literature study groups

National Geographic Society
School Publishing, P.O. Box 10041, Des Moines, IA 50340-0041, 1-888-225-5647, www.nationalgeographic.com/education
Range of leveled nonfiction books for guided and independent reading; content related topics; classroom magazine

Newbridge Educational Publishing

P.O. Box 800, Northborough, MA 01532, 1-800-867-0307, www.newbridgeonline.com
Range of books for shared, guided, and independent reading; many content area subject titles

Okapi Educational Materials

P.O. Box 2559, San Marcos, CA 92079-2559, 1-866-652-7436, www.myokapi.com
Fiction and nonfiction guided reading books; biographies; range of levels and content related topics

Pacific Learning

15342 Graham Street, Huntington Beach, CA 92649-1111, 1-800-279-0737, www.pacificlearning.com
Variety of fiction and nonfiction books for guided and independent reading books; nonfiction overhead transparencies for shared reading; magazine format nonfiction texts; books that feature a range of text types, themes, and topics; readers' theater

Pearson Learning Group

(Scott Foresman, Modern Curriculum Press, Celebration Press),
145 South Mount Zion Road, P.O. Box 2500, Lebanon, IN 46052, www.pearsonlearning.com
Large variety of fiction and nonfiction books for guided, independent, and literature study groups; many high interest leveled nonfiction books that support science and social studies content topics; Developmental Reading Assessment, Second Edition (DRA2), K-8

Perfection Learning

1000 North Second Avenue, P.O. Box 500, Logan, IA 51546-0500, 1-800-831-4190, www.perfectionlearning.com
Variety of leveled fiction and nonfiction guided reading; classroom library book collections; intervention high interest selections

Random House

1745 Broadway, New York, New York 10019, 1-800-733-3000, www.randomhouse.com
Many series books range from easy beginning chapter-type texts to longer more challenging texts for guided and independent reading

Richard C. Owen Publishers, Inc.

P.O. Box 585, Katonah, NY 10536, 1-800-262-0787, www.RCOwen.com
Fiction and nonfiction guided reading books grades 1–4

Rigby

Harcourt Achieve, 6277 Sea Harbour Drive, Orlando, FL 32887, Attn: Customer Service, 5th Floor, 1-800-531-5015, www.rigby.com
Large variety of fiction and nonfiction books for guided, independent, and literature study groups

Rosen Classroom Books and Materials

29 East 21st Street, New York, NY 10010, 1-800-237-9932, www.rosenclassroom.com
Variety of leveled nonfiction books for guided and independent reading; many content related topics; graphic-novel style nonfiction biographies

Rourke Classroom Resources

P.O. Box 3328, Vero Beach, FL 32964, 1-800-380-2289, www.rourkeclassroom.com
Variety nonfiction books for guided and independent reading; many content related topics

Scholastic, Inc.
557 Broadway, New York, NY 10012, 1-800-724-6527, www.scholastic.com
Large variety of fiction and nonfiction books for guided, independent, and
literature study groups; offer leveled texts; many content related topics;
classroom library book collections; intervention high-interest selections

Sunburst Technology & Tenth Planet Communications
1550 Executive Drive, Elgin, IL 60123, 1-800-321-7511 ,www.sunburst.com
Multi-media language arts software for K-12 grades

Sundance
One Beeman Road, P. O. Box 740, Northborough, MA 01532-0740, 1-800-343-8204,
www.sundancepub.com
Variety fiction and nonfiction guided and independent reading books; series
books; classroom library collections

Wright Group/McGraw-Hill
220 East Danieldale Road, De Soto, TX 75115, 1-800-648-2970, www.WrightGroup.com
Range of leveled fiction and nonfiction books to support guided, independent,
and literature study groups; intervention high interest selections

Magazines, Theme Books, and Newspapers for Intermediate Grades

Consider the following magazines, theme books, and newspapers as good sources for
short texts for guided reading and the classroom library.

Cobblestone Publishing
Division of Carus Publishing Company, 30 Grove Street, Suite C,
Peterborough, NH 03458, www.cobblestonepub.com
Cobblestone publishing offers a variety of topics and contents in these magazines.

Ages 7–10
> *Spider*: short fiction, articles, activities
> *Ask*: arts and science
> *Appleseeds*: history and cultures

Ages 9 and up
> *Cricket*: fiction, illustrations, articles
> *Calliope*: explore world history
> *Cobblestone*: discover U.S. history
> *Dig*: archaeology
> *Faces*: people, places, and cultures
> *Muse*: eclectic mix of science topics
> *Odyssey*: adventures in science

Cousteau Kids
Cousteau Society, 710 Settlers Landing Road, Hampton, VA 23669, www.cousteaukids.org

Kids Discover
149 Fifth Ave., New York, NY 10010, www.kidsdiscover.com

National Geographic Society

School Publishing, P.O. Box 10597, Des Moines, IA 50340-0597, www.ngschoolpub.org

> **National Geographic Explorer** (Pioneer and Pathfinder Editions); content and topics same in both editions, reading level varies
>
> **National Geographic Kids**

Ranger Rick

National Wildlife Federation, 11100 Wildlife Center Dr., Reston, VA 20190-5362, www.nwf.org

Scholastic Inc.

P.O. Box 3710, Jefferson City, MO 65102-9957, www.scholastic.com

> **Jr. Scholastic**
>
> **Scholastic News** Grades 3, 4, 5/6
>
> **Storyworks Magazine** Grades 3–6
>
> **Super Science Magazine** Grades 3–6

Sports Illustrated for Kids

Avenue of the Americas, 3rd Floor, New York, NY 10020, www.sikids.com

Stone Soup

P.O. Box 83, Santa Cruz, CA 95063, www.stonesoup.com

Stories, poems, book reviews and beautiful illustrations by young writers and artists ages 8 to 13

TIME For Kids

1271 6th Avenue, 22nd floor, New York NY 10020, www.timeforkids.com

U.S. Kids

Children's Better Health Institute, 1100 Waterway Blvd., Indianapolis, IN 46202, www.cbhi.org

Weekly Reader

Weekly Reader Corporation, 3001 Cindel Drive, Delran, NJ 08075, www.weeklyreader.com

Zillions Consumer Report for Kids magazine becomes Consumer Reports Online for kids www.zillions.org

Zoobooks

Wildlife Education, Ltd., 12233 Thatcher Court, Poway, CA 92064-6880, www.zoobooks.com

Databases

Many public libraries subscribe to a number of online databases that include thousands of publications. You can access articles, stories, biographies, reports, documents, and other types of information online. All you need is a library card number when you log on to the public library Web site!

Shaping Strategic Readers:
Summary of Behaviors and Instructional Possibilities

Reading is a complex, multifaceted process in which readers draw on a system of strategies to construct meaning. You may want to refer to this chart when reflecting on your students' reading behaviors and planning for instruction.

Reading Habits and Attitudes

- Self-selects just right books
- Reads a variety of genres
- Enjoys reading
- Has favorite authors and/or reading interests
- Makes time to read
- Reads a lot
- Reads for a sustained amount of time
- Keeps track of reading
- Talks and writes about reading
- Takes care of books

Reading Strategies

- Uses a range of fix-up strategies for decoding and understanding the meaning of words
- Detects and corrects errors
- Searches text for relevant information to problem solve
- Checks to make sure what is read makes sense, sounds right, and looks right
- Monitors for meaning
- Monitors for language structure
- Monitors for visual information
- Confirms by rereading or searching text
- Searches to locate specific information

Comprehension Strategies

- Uses background knowledge
- Makes logical predictions based on prior knowledge and previewing
- Makes connections (self, texts, world)
- Asks questions before, during, and after reading
- Creates visual images
- Makes inferences
- Determines importance
- Identifies key vocabulary
- Uses context clues to figure out vocabulary
- Summarizes
- Synthesizes
- Analyzes
- Evaluates and Critiques

Word Solving Analysis

- Uses beginning, ending, medial sounds
- Uses known word parts when problem solving
- Able to break word at difficulty into the largest possible chunk
- Solves unknown words by analogy from known words
- Has a large core of high frequency words and is able to read them fast
- Recognizes root words, prefixes and suffixes
- Identifies key vocabulary
- Uses context clues to figure out vocabulary

Oral Reading Behaviors During Oral Reading

- Omits words
- Substitutes meaningful words
- Repeats words
- Inserts words or phrases
- Appeals for words
- Over relies on one source of information (meaning, structure or visual information)
- Non-verbal reactions (laugh, smile)

The Reader

Fluency

- Groups words in meaningful phrases
- Phrased and fluent reading that reflects rapid word solving while thinking about the meaning of the text
- Adjusts reading pace and style based on text difficulty and purpose for reading
- Reads with intonation and expression
- Attends to punctuation

Identifies and Uses Literary Elements and Devices

- Character, setting, plot, problem, resolution
- Techniques such as figurative language, foreshadowing, flashback
- Visual imagery
- Metaphors/similes
- Point of view

Identifies and Uses Nonfiction Organizational Structures

- Description
- Compare and contrast
- Problem-Solution
- Cause and effect
- Time /Order Chronological
- Directions

Identifies and Uses Nonfiction Text Features

- Table of contents
- Titles and headings
- Illustrations, photographs, captions
- Glossary
- Index
- Diagrams, maps, charts, graphs
- Bold-faced words, italics

Self-assessment/ Goal Setting

- Reflects on reading
- Evaluates and talks about own reading process
- Provides specific examples of use of strategies. May even refer to text to explain.
- Identifies some strengths and needs
- Sets attainable goals

Reading Level Conversion Chart

Grade Level	Primary DRA K-3	Guided Reading Levels (Fountas & Pinnell)	Upper Grade DRA Grades 4-8
Kindergarten	A-3	A-C	
1st	3-4	C	
	6	D	
	8	E	
	10	F	
	12	G	
	14	H	
	16	I	
2nd	18	J	20
	20	K	
	24	L	
	28	M	
3rd	30	N	30
	34	O	
	38	P	
4th	40	Q-S	40
5th	44	T-V	50
6th		W-Y	60
7th			70
8th			80

Guided Reading Lesson Plan and Record

Date: **Materials:**

Title of Text:

Level:

Focus: (What do you want students to learn or practice by using this text?)

_____

Purpose for this reading: (What do you want students to find out/learn in this particular text?)

_____

Introduction *Before* Reading: (Questions, new or unusual vocabulary, text structure or features)

_____

***During* Reading:** (Record or oral reading, discussion questions, tasks for early finishers)

_____

***After* Reading:** (Discussion, return to the text, follow up)

Students	Observations	Future Teaching Focus

Reflection and Evaluation

Daily Reading Log

Date	Title	Author	Genre	Start Page	Type of Book (E, JR, C)	Date

Keep a list of books you read daily. Write the title, author, genre, start page, and type of book (easy, just right, or hard). When you complete reading a book, write the date in the last column. If you abandon a book, write "A" and the date you abandoned it in the last column.

Daily Reading Log: *Here is an example of a daily reading log students use to maintain an ongoing list of books read throughout the school year.*

Quarterly Inventory of Reading

Name _____

How many books have you read this quarter?

How many books did you begin and then abandon?

What different genres did you try this quarter?

What was your biggest reading success or accomplishment this quarter?

What was your biggest problem you experienced as a reader this quarter? How did you solve it?

What have you learned about yourself as a reader? How will knowing this help you as you continue reading?

What goals (list 2-3) will you set for yourself next quarter?

Optional:

What would you like your parent or guardian to know about you as a reader?

What would you like next year's teacher to know about you as a reader? (end-of-year)

Quarterly Inventory of Reading: *Some teachers use the "Quarterly Inventory of Reading" so students can self-assess the amount, kind, and quality of reading each they have done each quarter.*

Individual Reading Conference Class Record Sheet

Student Name	M	T	W	Th	F	Comments

General Observations/Possible Mini-Lessons:

Individual Reading Conference Class Record Sheet: *Teachers use the "Individual Reading Conference Class Record Sheet" to keep track of when they meet with students in the class for an individual reading conference. Teachers often list students' names alphabetically and reproduce the form so it is ready for use.*

Reproducible Bookmark to Collect Words

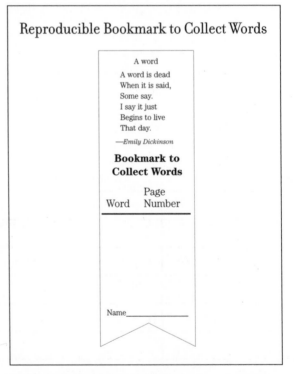

A word

A word is dead
When it is said,
Some say.
I say it just
Begins to live
That day.

—*Emily Dickinson*

Bookmark to Collect Words

Word	Page Number

Name_____

Book Mark(s)/Word Cards: *Students use a book mark or word card to jot tricky words during guided and independent reading. The teacher and the students can refer to words students have recorded on the book mark during both guided and independent reading.*

Professional References

Allington, R. (2001). *What really matters for struggling readers: Designing research-based programs*. New York: Addison-Wesley Longman.

Atwell, N. (1998). *In the middle: New understandings about writing, reading, and learning*. Portsmouth: NH: Heinemann.

Beers, K. (2003). *When kids can't read: What teachers can do*. Portsmouth, NH: Heinemann.

Brown, H., & Cambourne, B. (1990). *Read and retell*. Portsmouth, NH: Heinemann.

Brown, S. (2004). *Shared reading for grades 3 and beyond*. New Zealand: Learning Media Limited. Huntington Beach, CA: Pacific Learning.

Clay, M. M. (2001). *Change over time in children's literacy development*. Portsmouth, NH: Heinemann.

Clay, M. M. (1998). *By different paths to common outcomes*. York, ME: Stenhouse.

Cole, A. C. (2003). *Knee to knee, eye to eye: Circling in on comprehension*. Portsmouth, NH: Heinemann.

Cooper, J. D., & Kiger, N. (2003). *Literacy: Helping children construct meaning*. Boston, MA: Houghton Mifflin Company.

Cunningham, P., & Allington, R. (1994). *Classrooms that work: They can all read and write*. New York: Harpers Collins College Publishers.

Davey, B. (1983). "Think aloud: Modeling the Cognitive Process of Reading Comprehension." *Journal of Reading, 27,* pages 44–47.

Daniels, H., & Bizar, M. (2004). *Teaching the best practice way: Methods that matter, K–12*. Portland, ME: Stenhouse.

Fountas, I. C., & Pinnell, G. S. (1999). *Matching books to readers: Using leveled books in guided reading, K–3*. Portsmouth, NH: Heinemann.

Fountas, I. C., & Pinnell, G. S. (2001a). *Guiding readers and writers grades 3–6: Teaching comprehension, genre, and content literacy*. Portsmouth. NH: Heinemann.

Fountas, I. C., & Pinnell, G. S. (2001b). *Leveled books for readers, grades 3–6: A companion volume to guiding readers and writers*. Portsmouth, NH: Heinemann.

Hall, S. (1990). *Using picture storybooks to teach literary devices: Recommended books for children and young adults, Volume 1*. Phoenix, AZ: The Oryx Press.

Hall, S. (1994). *Using picture storybooks to teach literary devices: Recommended books for children and young adults, Volume 2*. Westport, CT: The Oryx Press.

Hall, S. (2002). *Using picture storybooks to teach literary devices: Recommended books for children and young adults, Volume 3*. Westport, CT: The Oryx Press.

Harvey, S., & Goudvis, A. (2000). *Strategies that work: Teaching comprehension to enhance understanding*. York, ME: Stenhouse.

Holdaway, D. (1984). *The foundations of literacy*. Portsmouth, NH: Heinemann.

Holdaway, D. (2000). Epigraph from "Schools That Work" a symposium at the International Reading Association, Indianapolis, IN, May 2000.

Hoyt, L., Mooney, M., & Parkes, B. (2003). *Exploring informational texts: From theory to practice*. Portsmouth, NH: Heinemann.

Hoyt, L. (2002). *Make it real: Strategies for success with informational texts*. Portsmouth, NH: Heinemann.

Hoyt, L. (2000). *Snapshots: Literacy minilessons up close*. Portsmouth, NH: Heinemann.

Hoyt, L., et al. (2005). *Spotlight on comprehension: Building a literacy of thoughtfulness*. Portsmouth, NH: Heinemann.

Huck, C., Helper, S., & Hickman, J. (1993). *Children's literature in the elementary school*. Fort Worth, TX: Harcourt Brace Jovanovich.

Keene, E., & Zimmermann, S. (1997). *Mosaic of thought: Teaching comprehension in a readers' workshop.* Portsmouth, NH: Heinemann.

Johnston, P. (2004). *Choice words: How our language affects children's learning.* Portland, ME: Stenhouse.

Krashen, S. (2004). *The power of reading: Insights from the research.* Portsmouth, NH: Heinemann.

Learning Media, Ministry of Education. (1997). *Reading for life: The learner as reader.* Wellington, New Zealand: Ministry of Education. Katonah, NY: Richard C. Owen.

Marzano, R., Pickering, D., & Pollock, J. (2001). *Classroom instruction that works: Research-based strategies for increasing student achievement.* Alexandria, VA: Association for Supervision and Curriculum Development.

Moline, S. (1995). *I see what you mean.* York, ME: Stenhouse.

Mooney, M. (1990). *Reading to, with, and by children.* Katonah, NY: Richard C. Owen.

Mooney, M. (2001). *Text forms and features: A resource for intentional teaching.* Katonah, NY: Richard C. Owen.

Parkes, B. (2000). *Read it again! Revisiting shared reading.* Portland, ME: Stenhouse.

Payne, C. D. (2005). *Shared reading for today's classroom.* New York: Scholastic.

Peterson, Ralph. (1992). *Life in a crowded place: Making a learning community.* Portsmouth, NH: Heinemann.

Rief, L., & Barbieri, M. (Eds.). (1995). *All that matters: What is it we value in school and beyond?* Portsmouth, NH: Heinemann.

Rhodes, Lynn, & Nathenson-Mejia, S. (1992). Anecdotal records: A powerful tool for ongoing literacy assessment. *The Reading Teacher, 45*(7): 502–509.

Rosenblatt, L. (1938; Rev. ed., 1983). *Literature as exploration.* New York: Modern Language Association.

Rosenblatt, L. (1978; Rev. ed., 1994). *The reader, the text, the poem: The transactional theory of the literary work.* Carbondale, IL: Southern Illinois University Press.

Routman, R. (2003). *Reading essentials: The specifics you need to teach reading well.* Portsmouth, NH: Heinemann.

Schulman, M. B., & Payne, C. D. (2000). *Guided reading: Making it work.* New York: Scholastic.

Serafini, F. (2004). *Lessons in comprehension: Explicit instruction in the reading workshop.* Portsmouth, NH: Heinemann.

Serafini, F. (2001). *The reading workshop: Creating space for readers.* Portsmouth, NH: Heinemann.

Sibberson, F., & Szymusiak, K. (2003). *Still learning to read.* Portland, ME: Stenhouse.

Stead, T. (2005). Comprehending nonfiction: Using guided reading to deepen understandings. In L. Hoyt, et al., *Spotlight on comprehension: Building a literacy of thoughtfulness.* Portsmouth, NH: Heinemann.

Tovani, Cris. (2000). *I read it, but I don't get it.* Portland, ME: Stenhouse.

Vygotsky. L. (1978). *Mind in society: The development of higher psychological processes.* Cambridge, MA: Harvard University Press.

Vygotsky. L. (1962). *Thought and Language.* Cambridge, MA: M.I.T. Press.

Wiggins, G., & McTighe, J. (1998). *Understanding by design.* Alexandria, VA: Association for Supervision and Curriculum Development.

Wilde, S. (2000). *Miscue analysis made easy: Identifying and building on student strengths.* Portsmouth, NH: Heinemann.

Wilhelm, J. (2001). *Improving comprehension with think-aloud strategies.* New York: Scholastic.

Wilhelm, J., Baker, T., & Dube, J. (2001). *Strategic Reading: Guided students to lifelong literacy 6–12.* Portsmouth, NH: Heinemann.

Wood, D. (1988; Rev. ed., 1998). *How children think and learn: The social contexts of cognitive development.* Malden, MA: Blackwell Publishers Ltd.